www. global

Inside the
HTML
browsing Internet MP3
service provider
hackers newsgroups

Sandra Muller
Jeff Queneau

CASSELL&CO

At the dawn of the new millennium there were

200

million Internet users in the world. 21

56,000 bps - the *current standard* for modem connection to the Internet.

 72

84% of users say that they use the Net to look for **information** on specific subjects.

 90

Due to incredible growth in the volume of online information, the best search engines still only manage to cover about

20% of the Web. 78

Over **4,500,000** *Web sites at the start of 2001.* ▶ 34

An estimated **14 million Americans** *will be involved in online trading in stocks and shares by* **2004**. ▶ 29

Save 60% on your telephone bill *by making your calls over the Internet.* ▶ 41

Over **17**% *of children aged 2–14 use the Internet.* ▶ 90

97% *of Internet users use e-mail and related services.* ▶ 90

@ has become the symbol of the Internet, thanks to Ray Tomlinson.

▶ | 81

WWW – the World Wide Web is a global network.

△ | 18

All e-mail addresses are shown in the following way: name@server.extension.

30

The average resolution of our computer screens is 1024 x 768 pixels.

Internet users can dabble on the stock exchange from the comfort of their own home. It is convenient, faster than buying and selling in the conventional manner and brokerage fees are reduced. 4,500,000 Americans trade on the Web, **12,800,000** monitor their investments, while **1,800,000 use** the Web to seek information and advice. At the start of 2000 approximately **1,300,000** Europeans were using online share dealing services. ▶ 29

Smileys or emoticons
Using punctuation marks to convey facial expressions, with a touch of humour.

 81

ICQ : I seek you
The Internet lets you use your keyboard to talk in real-time.

 100

Masters of the Internet
Are they really masters of the world?

 102

iloveyou, one of the more infamous computer viruses transmitted via the Internet in May 2000.

33

'You've Got Mail', a film that revolves around people's experience of the make-believe world of the Internet.

 105

51.3%

of Internet users are **English speaking.**

▶ 22

1969 :

Thanks to the work of **Vinton Cerf,** the computers at two American universities, located 500 km apart, were connected and an embryonic **Internet was formed.**

▶ 17

DISCOVER

THE INTERNET HAS BECOME THE WORLD'S LARGEST UNIVERSAL DATABASE
AND A MODERN PHENOMENON IN THE PROCESS.
SWEPT ALONG WITH THE MOOD OF THE TIMES AND
THE IDEALISTIC PRINCIPLES AT THE END OF THE 1960S,
IT TOOK OFF IN A BIG, BIG WAY, BUT WHAT IS LEFT OF THIS DREAM TODAY?
WHO CONTROLS THE NET AND JUST WHAT CAN IT DO?

What exactly is the Internet and is it different from the World Wide Web? These are perfectly natural questions for anyone who has not yet ventured into this particular brave new world. The term 'Internet' was coined to describe the linking up of individual computer networks. 'Inter' refers to 'international' and 'net' to 'network'. Hence the Internet is an international network made up of smaller computer networks all over the world. The term World Wide Web is often confused with the Internet, so that the two become interchangeable, but it is different. It is a system of finding your way around and accessing all the information stored on the computers of the Internet. The Web system works by using 'hypertext' links within Web pages. These can occur anywhere within a Web page and by clicking on them, you are immediately taken to another page of the Web. It is rather like reading a page of a book. You come across an instruction to 'see page 59' in the middle of a paragraph and instead of finishing the page you are on, you immediately turn to page 59 to see what it has to say.

THE CYBERWORLD

Thanks to the Internet, information technology has become more than a tool, it is a way of life shared by the entire planet.

The Internet is therefore a vast database of information that can be used by everyone, but it is used for far more than simply accessing data. Nearly every business card bears an e-mail address today and millions of individuals have got the bug and have personal e-mail addresses at home too. It has produced a complete revolution in communication in the short space of just a few years. However, e-mails are just the tip of the iceberg. The average user surfs the Net to do many things – download a film trailer for the latest Michael Douglas movie, buy some groceries, check out share prices, play a game, book a flight, listen to the radio, or simply look up the answer to a question that has been bothering him or her for some time. It comes as a complete revelation the first time a new user clicks on a hypertext link and is whisked away to another Web site that originates from a computer on the other side of the world. How else could you be transported from Weston-Super-Mare to the Amazonian forest via Broadway and the Louvre? Not to mention the excitement and sense of awe and wonder the new user experiences at the first sight of all the graphics, video and animation that is on offer. The Internet is certainly no shrinking violet.

'INVENTION' OF THE WEB

It is generally agreed that 1969 was the starting point, but the honing of the Internet into its current form took place, in stops and starts, over several decades. It seems that the precursor of the Internet made its appearance in the middle of the Cold War. The Russians had launched the first satellite (Sputnik, 1961) and the USA responded by forming the Advanced Research Projects Agency (ARPA). ARPA gradually abandoned satellites and space and moved instead into the field

of computer science. Two scientists were now to become major driving forces in the development of the Internet. One of them, Joseph Licklider, was affiliated with the Massachusetts Institute of Technology (MIT). He was passionately interested in computers and was one of the first to recognise their potential for everyone, being convinced that people should use information technology to pool their knowledge. He began his research at ARPA surrounded by the best experts in the field.

The next to take up the torch was Bob Taylor. In 1966 he financed the first computer network. There were three technical issues at stake – how to get machines to communicate with each other, the invention of a universal language so that computers could communicate with each other, and preventing breakdowns.

ENIAC (1946)
The first computer, developed at Pennsylvania University, practically fills an entire room.

The first two objectives were achieved in 1969. The first communication protocol (Network Control Protocol) was developed as a result of the work of Vinton Cerf, an American researcher, and President of the Internet Society. Meanwhile computer technicians were breaking up computer data into smaller 'packets' before sending it on to a host computer, in an attempt to avoid hold-ups on the network. This was the first example of a network protocol. The names of the technicians Frank Heart and Robert Kahn have gone down in history for their work on this project.

In 1969 American universities were allocated funds to develop network communication and the University of California and Stanford Research Institute (SRI), which were located some 500 km apart, were connected up and the very first, albeit embryonic, Internet came into being. They were very soon joined by other universities and by 1972 the network had grown to encompass some 40 sites.

Besides ARPA, an increasing number of organisations were now showing an interest in the Internet, in particular the armed forces and the scientific world. Development finance increased considerably. Each institution had its own network and protocols proliferated, due to the diversity of transmission methods and communication codes, for example, ARPANET (the name for the wide area network that served as a testbed for the development of the Internet protocols) and RPNET were transmitted by radio, whereas SATNET used satellite transmission. In 1974 Vinton Cerf and Robert Kahn perfected the Transmission Control Protocol (TCP), the forerunner of what is today known as TCP/IP, the protocol that drives the Internet today and enables computers to communicate with each other. It was during this era that the word Internet, a contraction of International Networks and also of Interconnected Networks, entered our vocabulary.

The World Wide Web was the brainchild of one man, Tim Berners-Lee, who studied physics at Oxford in the 1970s. He developed a computer system to help physicists share information stored on different computers and named it Enquire Within Upon Everything, after the title of a Victorian encyclopaedia. This was followed by a system on a much more ambitious scale, that linked physicists around the world using the Internet and formed the basis for what would emerge as the World Wide Web as we know it today. Driven by an idealistic vision, Berners-Lee was determined to keep his invention pure, away from commercial business concerns in order not to detract from the Web's purpose of facilitating the sharing of knowledge and so made it free for everyone to use.

THE ASTOUNDING SPEED OF DEVELOPMENT

The ability to be in different places at the same time should belong in the realm of fantasy, but modern science has brought this dream a little closer. The development of the Internet has been closely linked to the extraordinary development that has taken place in computer and telecommunications technologies. The speed and amount of development has been breathtaking. There is as much difference between today's computer and ENIAC, the first computer (1946), as between a Ferrari 40 and a Model T Ford. Nevertheless, only a few decades separate the two computers, whereas the Ford was designed almost a hundred years before the Ferrari. It is estimated that the power of computers has increased by 600 times over the last ten years, and that the same will happen over the next ten years.

Fortunately the car industry has not progressed in the same way, otherwise we would be driving vehicles with 6,000 hp engines. The arrival of the transistor (1948), then the integrated circuit (1958), and finally the microprocessor (1970) brought about massive changes leading eventually to the extraordinary degree of miniaturisation and proliferation of today's computer products.

At the same time telecommunications technology was developing at an equally astonishing rate. Contrast this with the history of the last two hundred years. Claude Chappe invented the telegraph in 1794, Alexander Graham Bell the telephone in 1876 and John Logie Baird the television in 1926, yet the Internet has shot into existence in a mere 30 years, quite an achievement. In Chappe's time it took over two hours to send a message from Paris to Marseilles. Today an e-mail can reach the other side of the world in just a few seconds.

THE WORLD WIDE WEB
The 'multimedia' Internet opens the door to an infinite number of Websites.

In the early 1990s modems (or modulator/demodulators, the devices that enable computers to communicate with each other over a conventional phone line) had speeds of just 9,600 bps (bits per second). These days the standard is around 56,000 bps, six times as fast. Other connection methods can make it even quicker to surf the net, ISDN (Integrated Service Digital Network) where the speed increases to 128,000 bps, and ADSL (Asymmetric Digital Subscriber Line) where speeds of 2,000,000 bps and above can be reached using an ordinary telephone line, and of course cable television. New technologies will enable

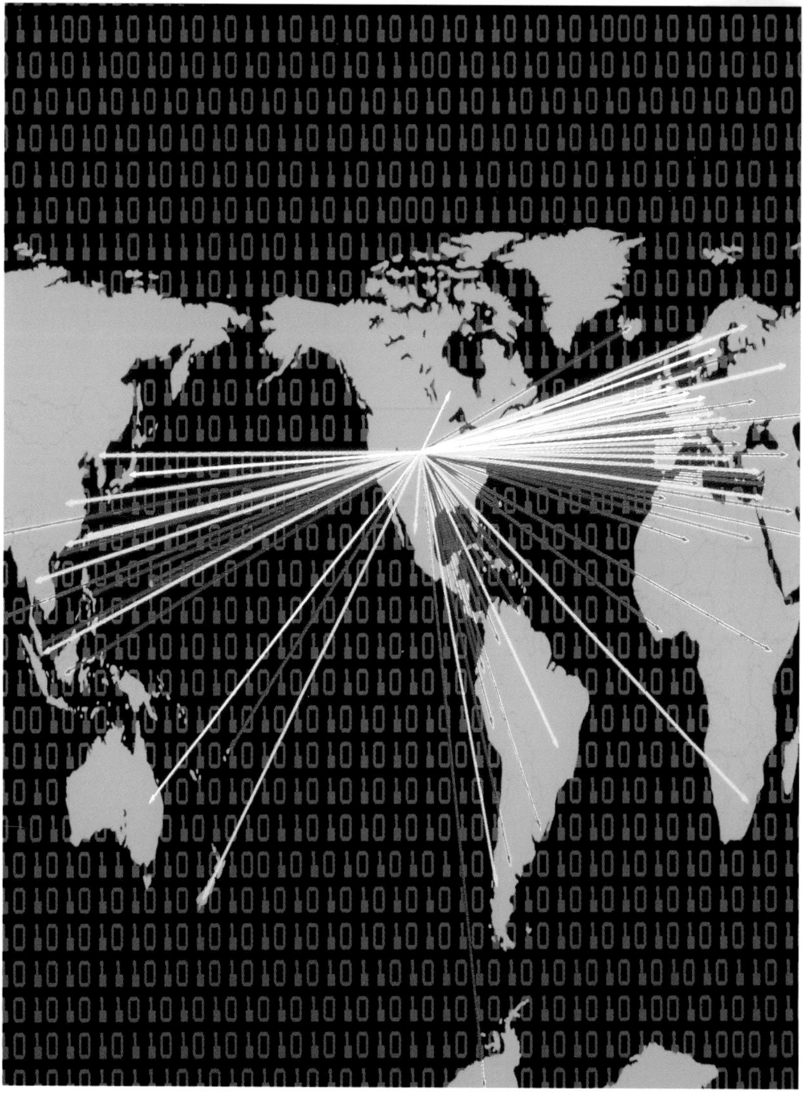

us to send more information at ever faster speeds. It is already possible to hold video conferences and download films, images, electronic books, music, in no time at all and with the greatest of ease, providing you have the right software and equipment.

THE WORLD IS OUR OYSTER

The Internet is the largest database in the world today, a sort of latter day Tower of Babel and Library of Alexandria in one, which can be consulted from anywhere in the world. Here, as well as exchanging knowledge and ideas, we can trade without barriers or limits of any kind. However, the adventure has scarcely begun – in the very near future the Internet will become even more 'mobile'. Using multimedia portable terminals we will be able to send or receive e-mails and remain logged on wherever we are. WAP phones, the mobile phones that enable the user to access the Internet, are already widely available and reasonably priced. Hardware developers are currently designing dedicated Web navigation terminals known as NCs (Network Computers). These are lightweight, low-cost machines (around £300) with no hard disk, available as either office NCs, portable NCs, with or without an integral telephone, or NCs without screens that plug into a television. These devices are thus truly portable, and perfect for users who are put off by the complexity of a normal computer. Manufacturers of traditional PCs have countered this development by bringing out the SIPC (Simply Interactive PC), a simplified version of the PC for logging on to the Internet. The stakes are high for all these companies – one of them may develop the machine the rest of us will come to use to access the Internet over the next few years. It goes without saying that whoever succeeds in this, will make a great deal of money.

INTERNET TRAFFIC

Map indicating the volume of information transmitted between the United States and other countries in November 1994.

MILLIONS OF USERS, BUT – HOW MANY MILLIONS?

There are millions of people who surf the Net, but the exact figure is difficult to estimate. For commercial reasons Internet Service Providers are not always honest about their customer base. Furthermore the statistical definition of an Internet user is not universally agreed. Is it a person who has logged on at least once over the last few months? Or someone who uses the Internet every day?

Market research regularly focuses on this issue, but estimates often differ enormously. The figures can be easily manipulated by promoters of multimedia computers bent on increasing sales or a particular Internet Service Provider with an enticing offer. However, it is still useful to look at a few detailed facts and figures in order to understand the extent of the phenomenon. There are an estimated 200 million Internet users in the world (source: *NUA*), that is approximately three per cent of a world population which has just passed the six billion mark. Predicted figures for the year 2005 diverge markedly. The *Computer Industry Almanac* estimates that there will be 720 million users, whilst *Datamonitor* (www.datamonitor.com) suggests 300 million. *Datamonitor*, however, bases its figures on a rather narrow definition of the Internet user as someone who logs on for at least six hours per week.

ENGLISH-SPEAKERS BREATHE A SIGH OF RELIEF

51.3 per cent of Internet users are English speaking (source: *Global Reach* www.glreach.com) and the Internet is an English-speaking arena. In November 1999 the United States, was home to over half of the entire world's Internet users, that is 110.8 million (source: *Computer Industry Almanac* http://www.c-i-a.com). It is predicted that there will be over 200 million Americans on the Net by the year 2005. Indeed in the United States the Internet has become a part of everyday life, bringing with it a socio-cultural transformation comparable to that which followed the invention of printing. In terms of communication, consumerism and work, habits have changed dramatically.

After the USA, Europe boasted 46 million Internet users (source: *Computer Industry Almanac*) at the start of the year 2000. But there are great differences between the various countries. The UK and Germany are in the lead with over 13 million logging on. Next are France, Italy and Spain. Russia appears to be under equipped; the most recent available data estimated that there were under two million Internet users.

THE ECONOMY OF THE PLANET

The idea of a world economy is becoming ever more meaningful due to the many Internet services now easily accessible from anywhere on the planet.

In Asia, Japan is way out in front with 19.3 million users, followed by China with 7.2 million and South Korea with 4.3 million. It is predicted that by 2005 the figures for China and Japan will shoot up to 37 million and 35 million respectively (source: *Computer Economics*).

The number logging on in South America would seem to be around ten million – of which seven million are in Brazil – and should reach 60 million by 2005, with Argentina and Chile in particular boosting the figures (Jupiter Institute).

African Internet Connectivity reports that the continent of Africa has approximately 1.5 million Internet users, of which one million are in South Africa.

A DEVELOPING NET ECONOMY

When considering the relationship between the Internet and the Third World, the debate centres around whether the development of new technologies is likely to accentuate North-

South contrasts and inequalities, or whether it may in fact reduce them. Developing countries are less advanced technologically and have far fewer existing infrastructures.

According to Nicholas Negroponte (Co-founder and Director of MIT Media Laboratory) and one of the 'gurus' of the Net, the Third World should be 'going digital' more quickly than some parts of the old world. People are not saddled with unsuitable equipment, and anyway the real impetus stems from a particular 'mind-set', not the available hardware. Hotmail, one of the largest Internet e-mail services to operate world-wide, was invented by Sabeer Bhatim from India. An international aid programme could help provide low cost telecommunications and computers and the developing world's population tends to be younger and therefore more adaptable.

The Internet has revolutionised the business world. Changes in our vocabulary describe the new socio-economic order; for example we use the term dot-coms to refer to the young innovative companies who offer their services at the 'click of a mouse'. An 'e' added at the beginning of a word indicates the 'electronic' aspects of an activity, hence 'e-commerce' for shopping and other financial transactions on the Internet. The traditional economy is adapting to take account of the new order dominated by the dot-coms. Most of the high street banks have now set up facilities online and many of the big supermarkets and retail chains offer armchair shopping with delivery. In the USA information technology accounts for a third of market growth. About 17 per cent of American households on the Net use it to make purchases, compared to 10 per cent in England.

NASDAQ

A Nasdaq advertisement in Times Square in the heart of New York – symbolic of the new economy.

THE NEW TECHNOLOGY HAS GIVEN RISE TO FEVERISH ACTIVITY

The stock exchange can experience either spectacular growth or equally sudden collapse, something that the fortunes of various dot-coms have illustrated very clearly. The market was for a time invaded by 'get-rich-quick' companies, with no great economic value on paper. The new Net economy generated an atmosphere of great excitement and near hysteria, that saw some dot-com shares double their value in a single day, but unfortunately some collapsed as quickly as they rose.

In the UK the online clothing store boo.com, one of the most hyped dot coms, was liquidated after a mere seven months trading (Nov 1999 – May 2000), after business failed to take off. Worth an estimated $200m on its launch, boo.com had amassed debts of $25m by the time of its demise. In the UK, Joanna Lumley's health and beauty venture clickmango.com suffered a similar fate, closing for business after one year.

Some Internet-linked businesses have been bought out for very large sums of money, Geocities bought out Yahoo! for $4.7 billion on the same day that Ford was buying out Volvo for $6.5 billion.

In just a few years Internet-linked companies have caught up with and matched the turnover figures of traditional industries, which have had to begin to focus on multi-media solutions to avoid falling behind. Partnerships between small and mammoth companies are on the increase, allowing the smaller firm to widen its range of expertise and operations under the wing and with the greater financial resources of the larger. The gurus of this virtual world, themselves very real indeed, are such entities as AOL – the first American Internet Service Provider (which has joined forces with the media giant *Time Warner*) – the big search engine Yahoo!, and the online commerce specialist eBay. The upward trend of stock prices in these companies was spectacular. Between January and September 1999, Yahoo!'s quoted value increased by 300 per cent, and it was the same story with eBay, the American e-commerce giant run by Margaret Withmann. Its market value increased six-fold in the space of four months and on the day the company went public, 24th September 1999, its shares went up by 163 per cent. The losses can be just as sensational. Take NASDAQ, an American stock market operation specialising in the new technology, which regularly undergoes wild fluctuations. Share values no longer depend on traditional criteria such as sales figures, new management or a change in organisation. A company's prosperity is determined by the number of people who log on to its site.

THE CYBER-CONSUMER – STILL HESITANT, BUT MUCH COVETED

The arrival of e-commerce has revolutionised consumerism. Cyber-consumers can eat, dress, do home-decorating and buy plane tickets on the Net. They don't even need to consult their diaries any longer, their computer reminds them when a partner's birthday is coming up so they can order a gift-wrapped present and electronic greetings card. Simple. Nor do cyber-consumers do battle with queues for the bus or the checkout, goods and services come to them. Life could be much simpler and less stressed. However, shopping online is still not a widespread practice, despite what you may be led to believe from all the column inches devoted to it in the press. There are two main obstacles to its expansion. Firstly the poor management of e-commerce services can reduce the time saved by shopping from home to virtually nothing. Websites are not always accessible when you need them, suppliers do not always deliver on time, or might even fail to deliver at all, and products found on the site sometimes turn out to be unavailable. Secondly it is still difficult to be sure that the Internet is secure. Encryption systems are reliable but there is still the theoretical risk of your credit card number falling into the wrong hands after you have made a transaction. To make small payments you can always use 'virtual money'. With this system the user pre-purchases an

E-COMMERCE

Its strengths – easy to buy goods and low prices, but growth will depend on improvements in encryption methods to make transactions more secure.

electronic purse containing a specified sum, from which amounts can be drawn as required. However, new high performance security systems are being introduced, such as SET (Secure Electronic Transaction) designed by Microsoft in association with Visa, Mastercard and American Express. There is also the new encrypting-modem, developed by French companies Com 1 and GemPlus. The Smart Card Security System is a small free-standing device, which plugs into a computer and authorises payment by card with complete security. New commercial practices are coming to light too, for example cookies, minute electronic tags implanted in our computers, give away secrets by recording the user's Web navigating habits. This can be helpful by enabling sites to anticipate the user's preferences when the site is revisited, though cookies carry some disturbing Big Brother connotations too. Some sites may pass information on to direct marketing firms specialising in customer profiling and preparing lists of consumers interested in certain types of product. These can then be sold on to companies with a service or goods to offer and so the hapless surfer becomes the victim of Internet junk mail, commonly known as 'spam'. Early in the year 2000, four lawsuits were filed against the American company *DoubleClick* in the USA in the space of a fortnight for having compiled a massive database on the activities and habits of Internet users based on information provided by cookies.

PLAYING THE MARKET ONLINE

Another activity that Internet users can practice online is dabbling on the stock exchange, a privilege previously reserved for the affluent. In this way people who may previously have been put off by the rather elitist aura of playing the market, or the task of finding a broker, can dabble too from the comfort of their own home. It is convenient, faster than buying and selling in the conventional manner and perhaps most significantly, brokerage fees are reduced. A recent *Dataquest* study found that 4,500,000 Americans trade on the Web, 12,800,000 monitor their investments and 1,800,000 use the Web to seek information and advice. At the start of year 2000 approximately 1,300,000 Europeans were using online share dealing services. According to a study by the American institute *Forrester Research* there will be 14,000,000 Americans doing the same by 2004. In addition to online trading, a whole host of other financial transactions are available via the Internet – from current bank accounts to mortgages and insurance. It is certainly convenient to check your account and pay bills from home and this appears to be the way banking is heading. The big clearing banks are notoriously closing high street branches, encouraging customers to bank online, and it can certainly be cheaper this way for the consumer, though to draw out cash, you still have to make a trip to a bank or 'hole-in-the-wall' machine.

ONLINE
Online services mean that individuals can be as well informed as professionals.

THE RISE AND RISE OF ELECTRONIC MAIL

E-mail is so simple to use that it has restored our taste for written correspondence, though some people feel that it is also resulting in a deterioration in standards of written English. For some reason, perhaps the informality of the whole thing, mistakes seem less serious than in a letter and the format encourages abbreviation. Whatever it is doing to our mother tongue, we have taken to tapping away at the keyboard with gusto and sending messages by the boatload. There is no need to go to the post box, delivery time is much reduced, e-mails generally reach the correspondent's mailbox in a matter of minutes, often just seconds, and the cost is minimal (just the price of the telephone call between computer and server). Such ease of use explains the fantastic success of e-mail. In contrast Internet users have nicknamed the conventional postal service 'snail mail'.

E-mail is the most popular service on the Internet. In fact some people subscribe for the sole purpose of having a mailbox. Your mailbox and address are supplied by your Internet Service Provider or ISP. When you send a message, it is stored on your correspondent's 'server' computer. Your correspondent logs on and looks for your message in their mailbox, and vice-versa. There are various types of e-mail software available (Eudora, Netscape, Messenger, Outlook, Pegasus …) which make it easy to manage your mail. All addresses are based on the formula: name@server.extension. The name is that of the subscriber, but as some names are very common, initials are often added, for example xysmith. The symbol @, means 'at'. 'Server' refers to the name of the computer in which your mail box resides; usually it is the name of your service provider, for example Freeserve, AOL, Madasafish, Compuserve. Finally the 'extension' indicates domain names which traditionally indicate your country (such as .uk for the United Kingdom, .fr for France, .ch for Switzerland, .de for Germany), or the type of organisation dealing with your e-mail (.com for commercial sites, .org for non-commercial organisations). In 2001, a number of new more specific domain extensions are set to be introduced, for example .tv and .shop, .ltd.uk and .plc.uk for limited companies.

e-MAIL
The Internet was not primarily intended for correspondence but the speed of e-mail has made this aspect increasingly popular, either through virtual noticeboards or in real time.

ATTACH ME – WITH CAUTION

When you send an e-mail you can add a longer text document, a picture or even an audio or video file by sending them as attachments to your message. The file will be sent with the e-mail message into your correspondent's mailbox, where it may be read using suitable software. The time required to download a file depends on its size and complexity. For example, a high resolution picture or a video clip may take ten or 20 minutes to download over a slow modem connection.

Compression software is available for sending large files in order to reduce the transmission time as well as storage space on your computer. Some ISPs limit mailbox storage capacity and it is worth enquiring about this if you anticipate being sent large or complicated file attachments.

Finally, it should be noted that e-mails can spread viruses. One of the most infamous was the *Melissa* virus, which contaminated millions of computers in 1999. When the recipient opened the file attached to the *Melissa* e-mail, it caused the same message to be sent to the first fifty people in the recipient's virtual address book, and so on ad infinitum. Although it did not do damage to users' computers, it is easy to imagine the colossal traffic jams created in the networks as a result. In May 2000 the *iloveyou* virus caused much greater damage because of its ability to destroy graphics and audio files saved on a computer's hard disk. Almost all large organisations and companies were affected; the CIA, the FBI and Microsoft all lost data. Television channels were victims too, finding that material that had been stored in computers had just vanished into the ether. The damage was estimated to be $5 billion dollars. Like *Melissa*, *iloveyou* was transmitted via e-mail. There is nothing that can guarantee a virus-free computer. The best advice is to install recent anti-virus software (such as Norton Anti-virus or PC-cillin), and to be cautious when it comes to unexpected messages. The golden rule is, don't open any message if you are unsure about its origins, and don't open or run an attachment that you were not expecting to receive, even if it appears to come from a friend.

NEWSGROUPS – GLOBAL MEETING PLACES

Forums or Newsgroups are the park benches, pubs and clubs of the Internet, where people meet to chat, share common interests and ask for help or information on any given subject. There are thousands of them, each devoted to a different topic. Each Internet Service Provider has its own selection and subscribers can choose which groups they want to belong to. Each discussion group is like a notice board on which people post messages, to which other people can reply. If someone has a specific question, they can post it and expect to receive several answers from other members of the group within just a few hours. Newsgroups can therefore very often provide much more targeted information and answers to questions than search engines. In most cases a moderator (someone who takes on the task of screening messages submitted), will be there to start, lead and refocus discussions. Users can also consult FAQs or Frequently Asked Questions to find answers to common queries or type in their own questions. This is a practice that is recommended since new members are likely to pose the same questions repeatedly and it can be very tiresome for regular subscribers to read the same question time and again. As in

NEWSGROUPS

One of the Net's strengths is that it offers the opportunity for immediate or deferred discussions on a very wide range of subjects.

other areas of the Internet, when you are posting a message to a newsgroup, geographical, generational and sexual barriers are well and truly torn down. The Internet has also become an arena for debate on world issues. A group of Chinese Internet users, for example, have used the Web to express their opposition to government regulation of the Internet in China.

Internet Relay Chat (IRC) is a 'realtime' variation on newsgroups. Users take part in a 'chat' where they can make live conversation, albeit in print only, with one or several other people. The largest of these chat channels is ICQ (I seek you) with about 40 million enthusiasts.

Three-dimensional IRC is also possible. Users appear in the form of little characters, 'avatars', graphic representations of people, who move around in a virtual setting. Messages come up on screen in the form of cartoon-type speech bubbles. This system might well be extended to many of the other virtual worlds to be found on the Internet such as electronic shopping malls.

DOES THIS PARAGON OF TECHNOLOGICAL ACHIEVEMENT HAVE ANY FAULTS?

There is a vast amount of data stored on the Web. It has become the largest database in the world containing thousands of books, hours of music and pieces of information. It would be impossible to compile a definitive list of all the Web sites in existence. New ones are being created every day. At the start of 2001 there were well over 4,500,000 sites compared to 100,000 two years previously. Most professional organisations have a Website – the press, radio and television channels, government ministries, universities, libraries, cinemas, companies and businesses, associations, etc. Data is often difficult to verify, and rumours spread like wildfire (see www.urbanlegends.com), but the Internet's most frequent shortcoming is out-of-date information. Regular updating of information seems to be one of the keys to success for Internet entrepreneurs.

THE WORLD'S RICHES
The Net's great strength is the vast amount of data it contains, interconnected by hypertext links.

HOME-GROWN AFFAIRS

Personal home pages, designed by individuals and often outlining their hobbies or interests, exist alongside the sites of organisations and institutions. These range from sites that might be termed serious, protecting the environment for example, to those concerning leisure pursuits. Fan club sites are veritable mines of information for people interested in celebrities, television, music and film.

Many of the most interesting sites are the work of enthusiastic individuals with no commercial motive. MP3, a format that produces CD-quality audio, came from amateur sites, and pirate versions of cult films are also available on line , though downloading these is of course illegal. At the other end of the scale, some businesses offer 'high-tech' Web pages (ultra fast access,

Internet

state-of-the-art graphics or video) which are often inaccessible to Internet users with less than state-of-the-art computer equipment.

DOES THE INTERNET CONSTITUTE A NEW MEDIA TYPE?

There is no doubt that older forms of media are also obsessed with the Web. It is a rare television channel that does not parade its expertise on the Internet, or radio station that does not pride itself on its online news, or newspaper that does not also have its reports, analyses and interviews on the Net. Cyberspace is being filled with the spirit of experimentation. Some radio stations re-broadcast their cult shows online while others owe their very existence to the Net (for example, Netradio.com, spinner.com). Broadcasting on the Net has certain advantages in that administrative responsibilities and financial input are kept to a minimum and, unlike the radio network, there are no geographical boundaries.

Television is becoming interactive, as broadcasters like the BBC use the internet to augment their programmes with further information and online discussions about recent programmes. Another key aim for television stations is to become a Web portal (such as www.beeb.com), encouraging the notion that they are public services and bringing increased traffic to their own Websites, or to adopt up-to-the-minute technologies such as terrestrial digital technology. This new method of broadcasting compresses a maximum number of channels into a single band to offer *à la carte* programming. Television is already preparing for this by setting up multimedia services. A few trail-blazers exist solely on the Net, for example the French language site Canalweb on whose programmes celebrated writers and politicians have made appearances.

THE MORAL CODE OF A COMMUNITY WITHOUT FRONTIERS

Almost 200 million people use the Internet to exchange messages and carry out research. They are part of a massive community with its own special language and signs (smileys) which flourish in newsgroups, IRC and e-mail. Poor spellers no longer need to stay in hiding since they have at their disposal an array of abbreviations, which can be decoded by the addressee. The anonymity of the Internet can give a new lease of life to the timid; fantasists can escape from the banality of everyday life, though it is also easy for the

VIRTUAL VILLAGES
The Internet fosters small communities of users who share common aims and interests.

unscrupulous to distance themselves from the truth. Parents need to be sure that the new friend their ten-year-old daughter has made on the Net is not in reality a forty-year-old man whose intentions may be questionable.

The Net has its own moral code, 'Netiquette', or rules for good behaviour. In newsgroups, for example, you would be ill-advised to post a message which is irrelevant to the topic under

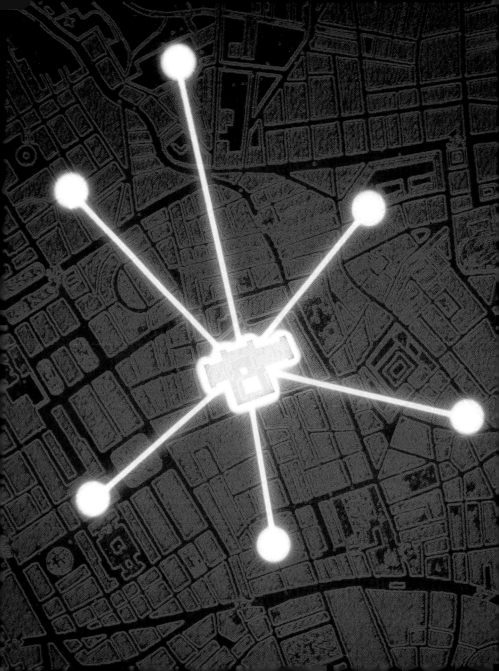

discussion as you would lay yourself open to the anger of other users in the form of flames (angry and possibly abusive messages), and typing in capitals is regarded as shouting. The moderator, if there is one, may censor inappropriate messages and throw out the culprit. One of the more drastic actions is to swamp the offender's mail box with very long messages with the intention of causing a blockage. As a last resort the Internet Service Provider may decide to suspend the offender's membership.

Sometimes virtual relationships develop into real ones and occasionally surfers travel around the world to meet up with their cyber friends. The site Respublica.com estimates that 10 per cent of its virtual community meet in the real world subsequent to a first contact in a chat room, and it is said that some Internet users even plan holidays around their virtual address book.

TELEPHONING VIA THE NET

If you have a multimedia computer, i.e. one that can display images, play audio tracks and animation as most computers can these days, it is now possible to make telephone calls on the Internet. Your computer needs to be equipped with speakers and a microphone, and the appropriate software, for example Internet Phone (www.vocaltec.com) or Netmeeting. The advantage of 'IP telephony', or Internet Telephony, is primarily its low cost. Whatever the distance between the two speakers, the conversation will cost (for each speaker) the price of a local call. The software digitises the voice, which is then transmitted in 'packet' compressed mode over the Net. At the other end it is decompressed and put back into analogue form. Callers are identified by their IP addresses. Currently the system does not function perfectly, partly because the PC was not designed for making telephone calls and extra audio equipment is needed (a headset and microphone). In addition, communication can be hindered by a busy network or a shortfall in the processing power of your computer. Voices can sound jerky and be difficult to understand. However, the situation is

INTERNET PHONE

Transmission in analogue form is still in its infancy.

improving as lines and high speed modems (128,000 bps and higher) give better quality transmission. Ideally the person you call should have the same equipment and software as your own, but if the person you want to call does not have a PC you can still call them on their ordinary telephone line, though you have to subscribe to a specialist operator to do this. There are many such services available. Two of the most noteworthy are Net2phone (www.net2phone.com) and iConnectHere (www.iConnectHere.com). You buy the special software and then buy so many minutes of calltime. The saving on long distance calls is around 50 per cent, compared with standard operators. You can also buy stand-alone phone devices

(www.aplio.com) which plug in between the telephone and the wall socket, and which transmit your call through the Internet. Both parties must have one. The saving in this case can be as much as 60 per cent.

This technology is likely to become very popular in the field of online commerce. It allows direct contact with the customer, making negotiation easier. Businesses also use 'voice over IP' within their own in-house networks, or Intranets, and this is where its use is most widespread currently.

GAMERS OF THE WORLD UNITE

The first network games were designed by American students in 1979. MUDs (Multi User Dungeons), role-playing games without any of today's graphic refinements, were wildly popular for a while, being easy to use and free.

These days the Web seems like a giant playground, frequented by a fair number of adults as well as children. A distinction has to be made between what used to be called video games, computer or console games that are supplied on a CD-Rom, and the games that you play on the Internet. The fascination of playing on the Internet is that it allows you to play in real-time against someone on the other side of the world, rather than just against the computer. You log on to the games site and away you go. One of the most well known sites is called simply the Zone (www.zone.com).

THE GAMING CYBERCULTURE

Some Internet users become hooked on interplanetary warfare, to the point that the virtual world becomes more important than the real one.

Internet gaming is not costly, there's no need to buy a CD-Rom, and you can play at any time of day or night if you feel so inclined. You will probably find someone in Australia who is raring to go at 4 am, even if the whole of Britain is asleep, plus the connection rates will be lower, for you at any rate.

As with PC computer games, a typical Internet scenario involves conflict of some kind. Imagine a universe made up of 900 million planets each inhabited by a different faction, as is the case in the game called Mankind (www.mankind.net). The objective is to defend your territory against enemy teams who threaten to colonise you. Each time they attack, whether you are online or not a warning is e-mailed to you, or you can even choose to be alerted via your mobile phone! In this parallel world you might choose to be a journalist, a builder of spacecraft or perhaps even an intergalactic James Bond. It is not difficult to understand why online players become hooked. Space is reduced to a manageable size, and the game is constantly evolving because anyone is free to intervene and change the parameters. You can download it free of charge or buy a more sophisticated version.

MP3 – THE HIGHLY CONTROVERSIAL MUSIC REVOLUTION

MP3 was developed from MPEG or the Moving Picture Expert Group, the name given to a group of technicians working on digital television in the late eighties. MP3 is a highly compressed audio format, which nonetheless offers near CD-quality sound. Because of the relatively small size of the files, it is easy to transmit, download and listen to on a computer, or even on a pocket MP3 player (similar to a Walkman). The first step is to download an MP3 player to your computer. The most widely known is WinAmp (www.winamp.com), but there are many others, for example Sonique (www.sonique.com), and Musicmatch (www.musicmatch.com). You can then download a piece of music from a site and listen to it on your computer, use MP3 to transfer it to a personal stereo, or change it into CD format ready to record it onto a CD-Rom. If you are a musician you can encode your own work in MP3 format and then put it on your own Website for others to listen to. MP3 has very rapidly become the industry standard. So where does the controversy come in? It is all to do with copyright. When you buy a CD, or tape, or listen to a track on the radio, a licence fee will be paid to the copyright owner. However, how do you ensure that such fees are paid when music is readily available to be downloaded from hundreds of different sites by anyone with the appropriate equipment? And what is to stop people taking a CD from their collection, recording it, and putting it out on the Net? There are two schools of thought. Those who view the Internet as an altruistic source of information and those who believe that each download should be paid for. There are legal sites, where music can be downloaded on payment of a fee, but equally there are many others that don't require a fee. Napster is a system that was invented by an American student. It does not offer music itself, but enables users to swap MP3 files by means of a sophisticated search engine and file-sharing of connected users' files. Again, it upset a lot of people in the industry because music was being distributed freely. This has now resulted in a court case being brought against Napster by A & M records, one of the US recording industry stalwarts. In March 2001, Napster was served with an injunction forcing it to co-operate with copyright-holders to stop specified files being traded online. Fewer files will be available to download and Napster will face trial on allegations of copyright infringement which may cost it billions of dollars, or even force it to shut down. It is also possible that collaboration with Bertelsmann may result in it becoming a commercial site, charging users for downloads. Napster is vulnerable to pressure from law enforcement agencies because, even though it doesn't store any MP3 files on its site, it does maintain lists of users and the files they hold. Other sites, such as Gnutella, don't maintain centralised user

LEGISLATION FOR MP3?

MP3 raises questions of copyright. A solution is still being sought.

databases of this sort. If Napster is unavailable (or if it is shut down), its peer-to-peer network won't work, whereas this wouldn't be the case with Gnutella. On the other hand, every time someone submits a request to Gnutella, it has to scan the computers of all users currently online, which means that searches are very slow.

The recording industry is naturally lobbying for tighter control on an activity which they say could quickly destroy the music business. However, although MP3 might cut into the profits of the big music labels, it could also act as a springboard for those who want to make their work known but lack the resources to produce a CD. A huge number of artists publish their music on the Net in this way.

SOHO, THE HOME OFFICE SECTOR

SoHo stands for Small Office Home Office. With the existence of PCs, especially lap tops, and faxes in the working world, it has been possible for some time now to work from home with ease. However, the arrival of the Internet and e-mail has made it even easier. Executives who in the 1970s would go off for the weekend with their briefcases bursting with folders, found in the 1980s that they only needed to take a few floppy disks and a laptop. These days they have their hands in their pockets as they set off for their little house in the country, where they have a computer linked to the Net to manage all their documents and messages.

WORKING FROM HOME
Relocating the office to the home was always a possibility with a telephone and fax, but has now become a more attractive option due to the services available on the Net.

For employers there is an economic benefit in that workspace is freed up and overheads are reduced. In addition, the cost of communication over the Net is very low and some employees are happier working at home for whatever reason. Nevertheless the system does have limitations as not everything can be done remotely using e-mail and the telephone. Direct contact is still indispensable for many situations and after all, body language is invisible on the Net.

THE COMPUTERISED HOME

In the near future, state-of-the-art technology may well transform our homes. Studies into the automation of the home and issues such as security, communication and energy management, are making great headway. Media One, one of the largest American cable operators, has already made plans for the house of the future. Soon our refrigerator, linked to a supermarket over the Net, will order the groceries – and universal protocols will mean that everything can be controlled through our computers. For example, to start a video recording we will simply click on the Internet code for video recorders, or if we want to see the participants in a particular meeting we will select the code for our firm's conference room. This is what the future holds according to Jim Parker, director of the Cool Town project at Hewlett Packard. If we have trouble remembering where we put the tea bags, we will simply ask our palm computer which will point us towards the right cupboard.

Just ten years ago we thought that television was there just to watch. Now we can link it to our computers to listen to music, play games and access Websites, or even access the Internet directly via the television (via a set-top box and a suitable ISP). Before very long the whole house and its equipment could be linked to the Internet, enclosing us in a cocoon of artificial intelligence that responds to its occupants and carries out their commands. It may even save us the bother of housework by cleaning itself. Fantastic! We will all be working at home, school will come to the children and our every move will be recorded on video ... but perhaps that is where this vision starts to get a little too '1984'.

THE INTERNET KITCHEN
Vilvoorde in Belgium. A futuristic house designed to demonstrate the possible domestic applications of the Internet.

WHO OWNS THE WEB?

Is it possible to monitor messages and images coming from the other side of the world? Is there an organisation that controls the Web? The answer is that no-one is in control of the Web, though a number of the major players in the field, such as Microsoft, AOL and Compuserve have played a considerable role in its development. In addition, independent organisations, such as the Internet Society which monitors technical standards and W3C (World Wide Web Consortium) which is devoted to setting effective industry standards, also play an important part. The running of each individual network within the Internet is the responsibility of each local network.

IS THE INTERNET TOO LIBERTARIAN AND FREE?

The scandal over pornographic pictures circulated by paedophiles encapsulates this question. Is it possible to establish where the films and photos have come from, and arrest the offenders? Is it possible to track down the children who have been violated and exploited in this way? The reality is that it is very difficult. Police responsible for monitoring paedophile activities are vigilant, but they are critical of delays in the passing of information between different countries and the difficulty in setting up investigations and instigating legal action. Another sensitive issue is whether ISPs are responsible for the contents of sites. Here again, opinions differ. In 1998 a young American sitcom actress Alyssa Milano was surfing the Net and came across some pictures of herself in the nude. Ms Milano did not appreciate the joke and started legal proceedings against the ISP. The actress's mother subsequently devised a surveillance system called Cyber Tracker, a service for celebrities concerned with their image, with subscription fees

of $2,000 dollars a month. Just a year later French model Estelle Hallyday complained about some very risqué photos of herself being circulated on the Net. Both the USA and UK, in independent but similar judgements, have implemented repressive measures whereby the ISPs are held to account for the sites they host. In the UK, Laurence Godfrey successfully sued Demon Internet (one of the UK's biggest ISPs) for hosting a newsgroup containing defamatory remarks posted by an anonymous impersonator. To avoid problems some countries have introduced total or partial censorship. In Saudi Arabia the Internet is filtered by servers in the Science and Technology Department, a state organisation, with a view to suppressing anything considered contrary to Islamic beliefs. In China those who surf the Net are expected to register. In North Korea the Net is simply banned. In Tunisia there are only two private Internet Service Providers, outnumbered by seven under state control, which restrict access to certain news sites. It is clear that the altruistic vision of the Internet as the facilitator of free information for all is more acceptable in some parts of the world than others.

HACKERS, CRACKERS AND OTHER CYBER-CRIMINALS

Today's cyber-criminals spend their time on the lookout for secure sites to infiltrate. They harass the authorities and are often untraceable. The fear that the contents of their hard disk are vulnerable to hackers or that an electronic eavesdropper might steal their credit card number is constantly lurking at the back of the Net user's mind. It is common for people to receive an e-mail circulated around a company or among friends advising users not to open a certain file as it may contain a deadly virus.

YOU'RE NICKED!
The new economy has added another area of criminal activity to be combated – investigating cases of computer-age fraud.

We should make a distinction between hackers, people who love to tinker with computers and the Internet but who mean no real harm, and crackers, paid-up members of the criminal fraternity. Ehud Tenenbaum, alias Analyser, one of the most infamous hackers in the world, went down in history when he broke into the Pentagon's security system. The authorities subsequently exiled him to Israel.

Several of the big sites such as Yahoo!, the online music and bookshop Amazon.com and the news site CNN.com were crippled in February 2000 after being bombarded with massive quantities of spurious data by a 15-year old Canadian hacker using the name 'Mafiaboy'. In the United States, the situation is getting so bad that ISPs are enlisting the help of the FBI.

Users of online commerce are understandably nervous about their credit cards – it is possible for a clever hacker to acquire a consumer's card number when he or she makes a purchase. However, when paying by credit card across the phone or even in person, the consumer is just as vulnerable to this kind of fraud. The vast majority of Internet sites use encryption systems which are very safe.

Hackers do not always end up on the wrong side of the the law or commerce, however. From time to time some are employed to help strengthen the security of a system which they had previously broken into. This fact has not escaped the hackers' notice and some, endowed with a sound sense of humour, have no qualms in leaving messages on large sites offering their services (with terms of employment and expected salary), together with the threat of a bug.

LEGAL SHORTFALLS

Most legal clashes relate to distribution rights for music and copyright, but there is another debate which sharply divides the opinions of Internet users, the issue of domain names. Here again the sprawling nature of the Web prevents any intervention on an international scale. In order to open a site and name it, the name has to be registered with the relevant body, but abuse of the system has thrown this free-for-all naming method into chaos. People or companies who were quick to buy up potentially desirable domain names have been able to sell them on at a handsome profit. A company or organisation will always want its domain name to bear a close relationship with its conventional name, for example, you would expect the domain name for the RAC to be www.rac.co.uk, which indeed it is. Imagine how irritated the RAC would have been if the name had already been purchased by some enterprising speculator, from whom they then had to buy it at a not insignificant sum, or, even worse, if the name was already in use. Contrary to this, recent court cases have shown that if a company has been trading for several years, they have certain 'intellectual property rights' over a potential domain name.

'BIG BROTHER' IS WATCHING

Will an electronic 'morality' manage to resist the effects of Web commercialisation? In its infancy the Internet brought together people inspired by altruistic ideals. Mercenary concerns could not have been further from their minds. They were driven by the desire for change and the excitement of working with this brand new technology. When the masses arrived on the scene it was of course inevitable that there would be movement in a different direction. Free information is losing ground in the face of profit-making services. The Net today may not have quite fulfilled the Utopian ideal of its founders. Nevertheless, it is a marvellous achievement that has revolutionised the world of communication in the space of a just a few decades and is still developing at an astonishing speed. A mine of more information than you could ever possibly need, useful, time-saving, and multi-purpose, it is also exciting and downright entertaining. So, log on and have some fun.

LOOK

THE WEB IS A MASS OF ABSTRACTIONS, FIRING THE IMAGINATION.
THE INTERNET HAS GIVEN A WHOLE NEW MEANING
TO A GROUP OF FAMILIAR WORDS.
THE FOLLOWING PAGES ADD A FURTHER TWIST TO THEIR INTERPRETATION.

navigate

Looking for information? Just indicate the general direction and the Web will guide you.

surf

Surf's up in cyberspace.

highway

Communication networks on the Web suffer traffic congestion too.

frame

Displaying Web pages containing several windows is an art in itself.

mail-box

You've got mail, thanks to your Internet Service Provider.

browser

Your browser works hard for you, visiting millions of Web pages and indexing their contents.

window

A window opens onto a Web page, which opens onto another Web page, which opens onto …

mouse

Explore cyberspace with your pet mouse.

world wide web

A vast network woven with hypertext links.

hacker

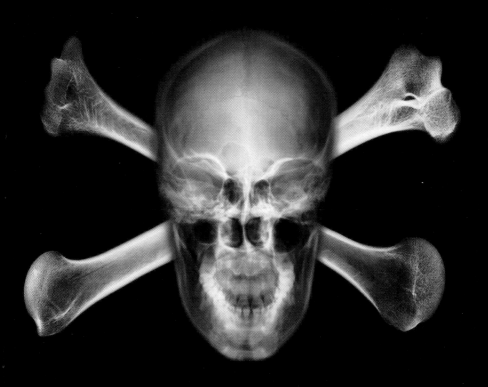

Beware, hacker at work.

home

There's no place like your home page.

village

gateway

To the information superhighway.

start-up

Great oak trees from little acorns grow – the parable of the Web.

buttons

Familiar and reassuring icon buttons lead the way from one page to another.

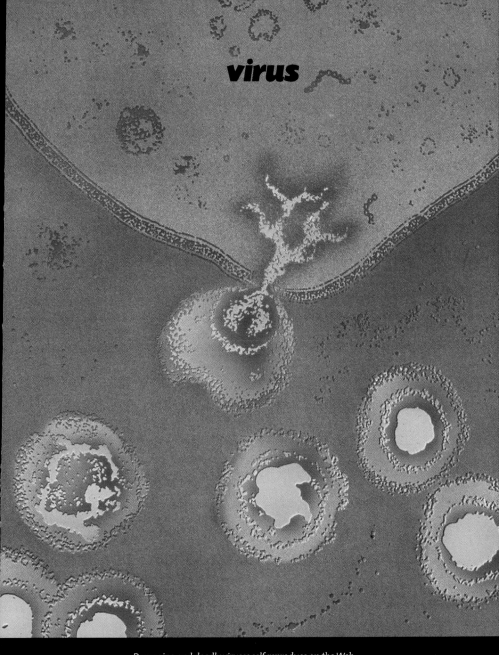

virus

Damaging and deadly viruses self-reproduce on the Web.

portal site

The portal is always open on the Web.

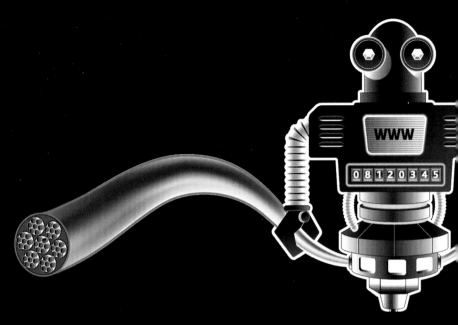

IN PRACTICE

THE EQUIPMENT YOU NEED TO GET ONLINE.
CHOOSING AN INTERNET SERVICE PROVIDER.
ADVICE ON USING E-MAIL AND PERFORMING AN EFFECTIVE SEARCH.
HOW TO DOWNLOAD MUSIC, PLAY A GAME ONLINE,
BUY A CD, OR CREATE A WEB SITE.
JUST SOME OF THE THINGS YOU CAN DO ON THE INTERNET.

Understanding networks

Expertise in the field of telecommunications networks will be one of the most crucial economic factors over the next few years.

Hard facts about networks

Most networks are interconnected.
Structure: Local Area Networks (LANs) connect users within one building or location. Wide Area Networks (WANs) connect them to sister organisations or external sites. Metropolitan Area Networks (MANs) provide connectivity within a city or conurbation.
Components: copper cables or optical fibre.
Transmission: terrestrial (radio) or satellite.
Language: digital.

Why do we need networks?

In today's world we have an unquenchable thirst for information in many different forms. Networks are the 'highways' along which this information travels, bringing us ever closer to achieving what is called global communication. The Internet (or 'the network of networks') is the cornerstone of this system, a sort of 'unifier' to which other networks are linked.

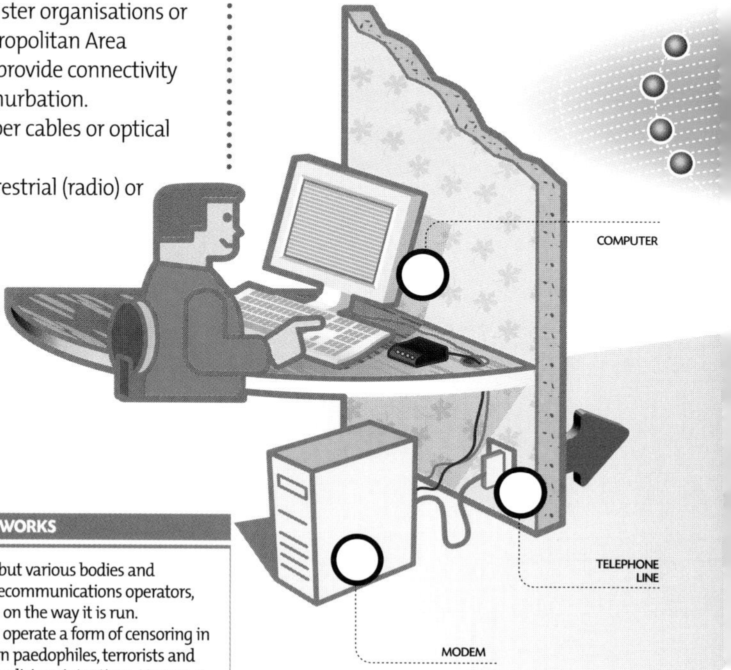

COMPUTER

TELEPHONE LINE

MODEM

CONTROLLING THE NETWORKS

Nobody controls the Net, but various bodies and organisations, such as telecommunications operators, can exert strong pressure on the way it is run.
Internet Service Providers operate a form of censoring in that they try to track down paedophiles, terrorists and hackers or crackers with malicious intentions. However, the system remains essentially uncontrollable.

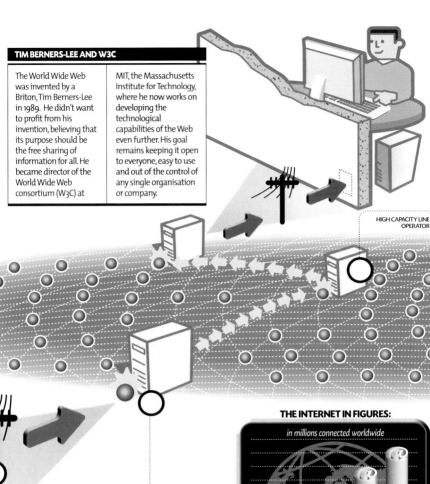

TIM BERNERS-LEE AND W3C

The World Wide Web was invented by a Briton, Tim Berners-Lee in 1989. He didn't want to profit from his invention, believing that its purpose should be the free sharing of information for all. He became director of the World Wide Web consortium (W3C) at MIT, the Massachusetts Institute for Technology, where he now works on developing the technological capabilities of the Web even further. His goal remains keeping it open to everyone, easy to use and out of the control of any single organisation or company.

HIGH CAPACITY LINE OPERATOR

THE ISP'S SERVER

TELEPHONE, CABLE, OPTICAL FIBRE OR SATELLITE INFRASTRUCTURES

THE INTERNET IN FIGURES:

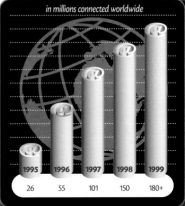

in millions connected worldwide

1995	1996	1997	1998	1999
26	55	101	150	180+

Choosing a computer and modem

Two pieces of equipment, or hardware, are required in order to navigate the Web: a computer to enable us to access and view data and a modem through which the data passes.

Choosing a computer: PC or Mac?

PCs used to outnumber Macs, though the latter have been making big inroads into the market recently due to their stylish appearance and some nifty marketing from Apple.

Advantages of a Mac: ease of use due to an intuitive operating system which hides much of the complexity from the user. Recent Macs such as iMacs and G4s have powerful processors, built in 56k modems and a search engine called Sherlock designed to make it easier to search the Internet or your hard disk. Macs are commonly used in graphics and media industries. The operating system (the computer's main programme that controls all the others) is Mac OS.

Advantages of a PC : a wide choice of brands and a wider choice of software than for the Mac. More peripheral options too. Various operating systems are available including Linux, which is powerful, stable and free, though Microsoft Windows is pre-installed with most PCs these days.

The computer's memory and processor

These days at least 32 MB of random access memory is required to navigate the Web, but you will need 64 MB or 128 MB if you want to take advantage of all the multimedia tools now available. Processors are the brains of the computer and range from the budget Celeron 500 MHZ to the Pentium 4 or AMD Athlon, which are now available with speeds of up to 1.5 GHZ. Powerful processors make it easier for more than one operation to be carried out at the same time. They can represent up to 25 per cent of the total equipment price.

The modem

Most modern PCs are equipped with a built-in modem (modulator/demodulator). It lets your computer use a conventional telephone line to log onto the Internet. It converts the digital signals sent out by the computer into audio signals, in order to be transmitted on the telephone network. The signals then have to be converted back into digital form upon receipt so that the receiving computer can understand them. o becomes a deep tone and a 1 becomes a high pitched sound. oo, o1, 10 and 11 each have specific frequencies.

SURFING THE NET SUCCESSFULLY

The quality of your equipment and how up-to-date it is affects your surfing activities. A modem's speed is measured in bps (bits per second), or sometimes kbps (kilobits per second) or even mbps (megabits per second). The first modems worked at 9,600 bps while the current standard is 56,000 bps. There are also modems available for new data transmission technologies: ISDN (Integrated Services Digital Network) where the speed rises to 128,000 bps, and ADSL (Asymmetric Digital Subscriber Line) where speeds from 500 Kbps to 8 mbps are reached. However, the quality of your Internet Service Provider's bandwidth may also play a part and at certain times of day, the Net is pretty congested. Users in Europe notice a marked reduction in surfing and accessing speed after around 2 pm (9 am in New York) as that is when East Coast America starts logging on.

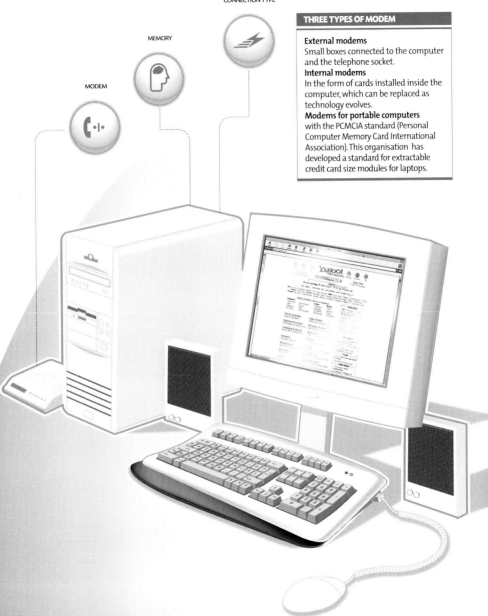

SPEED AND
CONNECTION TYPE

MEMORY

MODEM

THREE TYPES OF MODEM

External modems
Small boxes connected to the computer
and the telephone socket.
Internal modems
In the form of cards installed inside the
computer, which can be replaced as
technology evolves.
Modems for portable computers
with the PCMCIA standard (Personal
Computer Memory Card International
Association). This organisation has
developed a standard for extractable
credit card size modules for laptops.

Which Internet Service Provider?

An Internet Service Provider (ISP) provides access to the Internet. There are two kinds of ISP available, those offering free access and those charging a subscription.

What do they offer?

An ISP provides the subscriber with at least one, but often a number of e-mail addresses. When you log on to the Internet it is the ISP's home page that will be the first to download onto your screen. There is nothing to stop you registering with more than one ISP if you so wish, although this option is more likely to be the case if you choose free ISPs. This can be an advantage if you find Internet access particularly slow with one ISP as you can simply switch to another account.

A free ISP, or one for which you pay?

Some providers (such as AOL and Demon) charge their users a subscription fee. Others (such as Virgin and Madasafish) offer free access to the Net, a practice that began in the UK and has since spread to the rest of the World. Though it may be termed 'free' a free ISP does not mean you can surf the Internet for nothing. You will pay for the cost of the time you spend online at the local phone call rate. Free ISPs also tend to charge handsomely for their telephone support, should you need it. Recently, some ISPs (BT

access to their cable TV and telephone package at even more minimal cost. The newest development is the availability of ADSL connections, and ISPs are already offering services tailored to this new technology, although at present it is expensive, and coverage by no means extends to all areas. The range of packages on offer can seem utterly bewildering, but many Internet magazines publish reports rating each Internet Service Provider's advantages and disadvantages to help you choose.

and NTL, for example) have begun to offer so called 'unmetered' access, where the telephone charges are absorbed into a monthly subscription. This can be much more economic for heavy users. Users in areas with cable telephone lines can sometimes add free 'unmetered' Internet

EASE OF ACCESS TO THE INTERNET

Ease of access varies according to:
• The Service Provider's transmission bandwidth.
• The number of users the Internet Service Provider manages.
• The number of modems the Internet Service Provider has – to be able to respond adequately to simultaneous connection demands.

IF YOU ARE CHOOSING AN INTERNET SERVICE PROVIDER, FIND OUT ABOUT ...

• The monthly subscription fee and any special deals.
• The cost of international, national and local calls.
• Navigation speed.
• The cost of technical support by phone.
• The quality of the technical support – technical advice and hours of operation.
• Services: mailbox capacity, Website space, portals ...
• Look out for reports on the performance of different ISPs in computer magazines. They can be very useful in helping you make your choice.

Browsers

Navigators, or browsers, are programmes which let you access the Web and allow you to view its pages. The two main browsers on the market are Internet Explorer (Microsoft – pre-installed with many PCs) and Netscape Navigator (Netscape). Internet Service Providers often include them in their installation CDs.

Useful facts about browsers

• As in word processing you can 'cut and paste' and save images – useful if you want to copy something from a Web page into a document.
• It need not cost you much to browse the Web. Go to 'Work Offline' in Internet Explorer 5.0, or 'File','Offline' and 'Work Offline' in Netscape Communicator. You can therefore spend your time and money online gathering pages to read offline at your leisure at no cost.
• A Web address usually starts with the formula http://www, followed by the name of the site, a full stop and a suffix. http://, or Hypertext Transfer Protocol, is the way in which data is transmitted. www, or World Wide Web,

indicates that you are entering cyberspace. Website addresses have no capital letters or accents.
• Use the browser to copy a link address, create a new window with a link, add a bookmark, join a newsgroup, chat, send e-mail, play audio or video files …
• If you want to speed up your surfing, one option is to set your browser to just download text by turning off images and other multimedia aspects of sites as these take a long time to download. However, in doing this you lose a lot of the fun and appeal of the Web.
• If you are concerned about protecting your children from pornographic sites or undesirable material, you need to obtain software that filters out and bars

access to undesirable sites, such as www.netnanny.com, or encourage your child to use a child-friendly search engine such as www.a1source.com You can also restrict the type of sites viewed by altering the settings in Content Advisor in Windows where you can set the level of nudity or violence you will allow using a sliding scale.

The suffix denotes the country:
uk: United Kingdom
au: Australia
be: Belgium
de: Germany
dk: Denmark
or identity type:
com: commercial
edu: education
ac: academic
gov: government
mil: military
org: organisation or association
New domain suffixes to be introduced during 2001:
.tv: for broadcast and television-related organisations
.shop: for online shopping resources
.ltd.uk: for UK limited companies.
If there is no country code, the site probably originates in the USA.

BUTTONS
You can access key functions using the buttons at the top of the screen or options in the drop-down menus.

ADDRESS
A text box (known as location or address) into which you type the address (or URL) of the site you want to log onto. A typical address begins http://www.

LINKS
The main window is for displaying documents you have consulted. Underlined words are hypertext links that lead you to another Web page – position the cursor over them and it turns into a little hand, click and you are whisked away to another page. Links are usually underlined.

VIEWING A DOCUMENT
At the bottom of the screen a status bar tells you about the contents of the Web page displayed. Point the cursor at a certain spot and read the names of the relevant files. Here you can also see information on the current download status.

Search engines

The Web is like a complex of Aladdin's caves containing millions of pieces of information and this is where the problem lies. Just how do you access the one piece of information you require out of all the data that is on offer? Search engines are sites equipped with powerful computers to sift through data for you.

Search engines

Type in a word, or a phrase and the search engine will display a list of relevant pages thanks to 'Web crawlers', special software programmes which patrol and index Web sites according to the words they contain. The more precise the keywords or topic, the more precise the results of the search will be, for example, if you simply search using the word 'cars' billions of matches will be found, but if you type in 'classic cars' or 'Bugatti', the matches will be reduced to a more manageable level. Use a search engine if you are looking for a specific mention of something on a page.

Directories

Directories catalogue sites according to subject areas. They are particularly useful for finding general information, so use a directory if you want to look through a range of sites within a certain subject area, rather than for a certain item of information.

Search agents (or Meta Search Engines)

Several search engines are used at once and their results are combined. Therefore search agents offer you more relevant results. They avoid duplication and memorise searches already carried out in case they should need to be carried out again.

INDEXING BOTS

These robots visit Web pages and feed information into search engine databases. Despite the fact that bots perform increasingly well, the incredible growth in online data means that the proportion of sites they index is decreasing.

Useful addresses

DIRECTORIES
Yahoo
www.yahoo.com
Magellan
www.mckinley.com
NetSearch
www.netscape.com
Starting Point
www.stp.com

SEARCH AGENTS
Copernic
www.copernic.com

Meta Crawler
www.metacrawler.com
PowerSearch
www.stpt.com
ProFusion
www.profusion.com
Savy Search
www.savysearch.com
Ask Jeeves
www.ask.co.uk
Google
www.google.com

SEARCH ENGINES
Altavista
www.altavista.com
Fast Search
www.alltheweb.com
HotBot
www.hotbot.com
Infoseek
www.infoseek.com
Lycos
www.lycos.com
Northern Light
www.nlsearch.com

THE INVISIBLE WEB

There are thousands of online database resources now available as part of the Web, however these sites are often 'invisible' to conventional search engines and 'Web bots' as the information they contain is dynamically generated in response to a user's search request. Direct Search (http://gwis2.circ.gwu.edu/~gprice/direct.htm) and the lycos invisible Web catalogue (http://dir.lycos.com/Reference/Searchable_Databases/) are two resources which enable you to search the invisible Web.
Web rings are also available for reference.
A Web ring is a linked group of Websites which deal with a particular subject. The visitor can easily navigate from one site to another in the ring. Web rings usually have a homepage which lists all the linked sites, and gives general information about the topic of concern. They do not give any guarantee of quality or authoritativeness, being mostly run by keen enthusiasts who seek to propagate information about their areas of interest, hobbies, etc. Approximately 500,000 sites are organised in this way, with over 45,000 subject areas.

For initial consultation:
www.webring.org

e-mail: a communication revolution

In the United States, e-mail, or electronic mail, is on the verge of overtaking the traditional postal service in terms of volume. It is a highly convenient way of communicating – a few clicks of the mouse and a message is sent and received. Text, image or audio files may be attached too. The time taken to send or receive attachments depends on the size of the file, how much traffic there is on the Web at the time and whether the intermediate server computers are 'up', but 80 per cent of e-mails are said to be sent and received within five minutes.

Web-based e-mail

Have Web-based e-mail, will travel. It means that you are not tied to your own PC in order to send an e-mail. Type in your name and password and your mailbox is instantly operational. You can access it from any computer with an Internet connection, at work, at home or abroad. Hotmail is the best known. Other e-mail services, linked to an ISP, are termed 'standard'.

Practical advice

• Having several mailboxes with one provider but under different names can be useful if you want to distinguish personal messages from professional ones.
• Never open an attachment if you are unsure about it. It could contain a virus. Just delete it straight away.
• Give your messages clear subject headings, so the reader can deal with them more easily.
• In order to reduce the cost of being online, compose your e-mails offline, then log on to send them.

• Get to the point. This is common Internet practice and has led to a style of language that is uncluttered by traditional polite formulae.
• Use smileys to soften a rather direct message.
• Your e-mail address is private, but will be displayed at the head of each message you send unless you take steps to hide it (see final point).
• Tell the recipient what software is needed to open an attached file.
• Data compression/ decompression software such as Winzip for the PC or Stuffit for the Mac can be downloaded free. Use it to send large or complex items such as a picture to minimise transfer time.
• If you want to remain anonymous use a remailer like anonymizer.com.

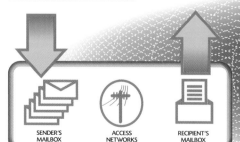

SENDER'S MAILBOX   ACCESS NETWORKS   RECIPIENT'S MAILBOX

Watch out for hoaxes!

Under the guise of a friendly e-mail message warning you about a so-called virus, a hoax message asks you to forward the warning to everyone in your address book. In these cases the virus does not exist, but a nuisance is caused by the build-up of Internet traffic as all the hoax e-mails are forwarded to millions of unsuspecting users.

To find out more:
www.europe.fsecure.com /virus-info/hoax/

Origins of the @ symbol

@, the symbol of the Internet, was adopted by the American Ray Tomlinson who developed the first electronic mail programme in 1972. He wanted to use a character which was not found in dictionaries, but existed on all keyboards.

SMILEYS, A UNIVERSAL SIGN LANGUAGE TO AID EXPRESSION

:-)	smiling	ʘ‿ʘ	#-)	gloating	♯
:-(	frowning	·̣·	:-#	mum's the word	♯
:-))	laughing	☺	:-l	indifferent	·̈·
:-((	depressed	☹	:-{	sulking	·̣·
;-)	winking	·̈·	:-o	shocked	○̈
>;->	mischievous	⚡	:'-(	crying	·̈·

MAILING LISTS

Mailing lists are just like conventional postal mailing lists. You put your name on one and are automatically sent messages by e-mail that relate to a particular topic. It is a way of being kept up-dated about something. They can be closed, in which case you receive messages only, or open, in which case you may respond and take part in a group discussion.

MP3: music on the Internet

Update your music collection via the Net and MP3, a digital audio format for transferring files over the Internet, which offers a small file size but high quality reproduction. Various sites offer information on the use of MP3 – try www.mp3.com. Or, if you are a budding Bob Dylan without a recording deal, make your music available on the Web via an MP3 recording.

Downloading

The first step is to download an MP3 player from the Internet. This programme will let you read MP3 files, or in other words, convert them into audible sounds. Use recording software to record the files on to a writeable CD to play back on your hi-fi or listen to them on a pocket MP3 player. Stereo systems already equipped with MP3 audio players are starting to become available. The pocket MP3 player stores the music in its internal memory (from 32 MB upwards), or on removable cards. It can generally be connected to a computer via a USB port. So-called 'Personal Jukebox' MP3 players are now becoming available, which can store much larger amounts of music (often as much as 300 hours worth).

Copyright and the law

It is virtually impossible to control the downloading of MP3 files, which is, strictly speaking, illegal if you do not have permission from the copyright holder. Some sites are legal providing both free tracks and those you have to pay for, but others are not. If you have paid for the files or obtained them legally, you are allowed to download and copy them onto a CD for your own personal use, but not to distribute them elsewhere in any way.

Memory cards

There are two types available: Smart Media, with a capacity of up to 64 MB, and Compact Flash with up to 128 MB. In addition IBM sell 'mini' hard disks with a similar format to Smart Media cards. These have a capacity of 340 MB. Half an hour of near CD quality music uses up about 32 MB. At present a 16 MB card costs from approximately £26

(Smart Media) to £35 (Compact Flash). However the price is likely to drop fairly quickly since the cards are used in many applications and are now mass produced.

WHERE?

A few sites where you will find MP3 links to let you download all the software you need, and of course, music.

Napster
(see p.42 for latest information regarding Napster)

Lycos
www.mp3.lycos.com
MP3.com
www.mp3.com
Multimania
www.multimania.com
Rolling Stone
www.rollingstone.com

Making phone calls via the Internet

Various software is available to allow you to make telephone calls via the Internet.
The most well known is Net-Meeting, which comes as standard with Microsoft's Windows.
For PC to telephone communication you will need to subscribe to a service such as:

Net2 Phone
www.net2phone.com
Aplio
aplio.com
BuddyPhone
buddyphone.com
Media ring Talk
www.mediaring.com
Soft fone
www.pak.net
VDO Phone
www.vdo.net
Video Vox Phone Gold
www.vox-phone.com
Virtual Voice
www.virtual-voice.com
Web phone
www.webphone.com

It is possible to transmit your voice over the Internet. In other words you can make telephone calls over the Net and take advantage of the low cost of being able to phone the other side of the world for the price of a local connection. The system is known as 'IP telephony'.

Equipment

• A computer with enough 'muscle' to handle the job (Pentium III-600 MHZ plus or the new Mac G4 based systems are recommended).
• A microphone and a pair of multimedia speakers. With a Web cam you can also take part in videoconferencing.
• A modem, preferably a fast one (56,000 bps). If you have a special ADSL or ISDN connection, so much the better.
• Suitable software, which can be downloaded free or purchased for a reasonable sum.

System compatibility

The person you are calling must have a configuration which is compatible with yours. It is also possible to make a call to a standard telephone using a service such as Net2Phone or iConnectHere. An alternative would be a standalone device such as Aplio which looks and works like an ordinary telephone but automatically calls through both the caller and receiver's ISP. The technology is still fairly much in the teething stage, so it may not always work perfectly first time. VOIP is a new technology that can be used for Internet telephony and is arousing a lot of interest at the moment. Other programmes are available, such as Net-Meeting (with Microsoft's Internet Explorer) and Conference (with Netscape).

CONNECTION TYPES

A Telephone to telephone
• Share the communication costs between the two of you.
• Use the same Aplio device as the other person.

B PC to telephone
• Use telephone software.
• Subscribe.

C PC to PC
• Use software such as Net-Meeting.
• Agree on a pre-set time to call.
• Have your conversation.
• Pay the price of a local call.

D The future
Based on the private networks of big multi-nationals, no specific equipment will be necessary.

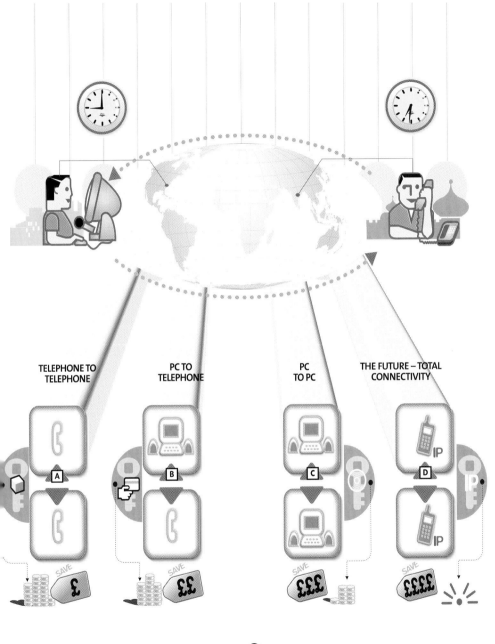

TELEPHONE TO TELEPHONE

PC TO TELEPHONE

PC TO PC

THE FUTURE – TOTAL CONNECTIVITY

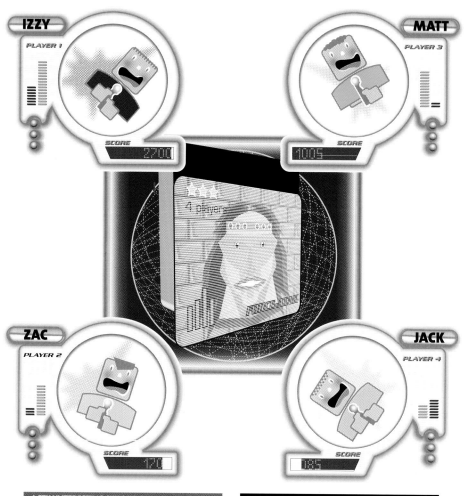

IZZY

PLAYER 1

SCORE 2700

MATT

PLAYER 3

SCORE 1005

4 players

000 000

ZAC

PLAYER 2

SCORE 170

JACK

PLAYER 4

SCORE 185

A FEW INTERESTING SITES TO GET YOU STARTED

www.multipathmovies.com
3D games where you can play the hero of an interactive universe
http://play.yahoo.com
classic games: poker, draughts, chess...
www.shockrave.com
specialising in adventure and action games
http://pbm.net.au
games via e-mail

GAMES FOR ALL TASTES

- role-play games
- simulation games
- adventure games
- action games
- war games
- strategy games
- card games...

Online gaming

From New York to London enthusiastic games players are able to go online at any time of the day or night and find someone to play against. In Britain we are now spending more on computer games than on renting videos and visiting the cinema. Each game costs around £1.5 million to develop.

How to play a game on the Internet

The 3D gaming universe needs to be set up specially. Each game has its own downloadable software enabling you to move around among virtual images. Download time varies depending on your computer's processing speed and the programme you are installing. The game may contain video images and sound for which you will need a fair amount of memory.

Technological developments are feeding the current passion for online gaming, response time is constantly being reduced, bringing the gaming experience closer to real-life conflict situations.

Cut-down or less powerful versions are often readily available. One example is Mankind, a gigantic role play game. The basic version of this is available free, but you have to pay to add more sophisticated options. In most cases you have to give your credit card number to be able to take part in good online games. Some games also require the support of a CD-Rom.

The future of the CD-Rom game

Producers are adapting to the online gaming trend by working on cut-down versions of games that are currently supplied on CD-Rom to be directly accessible via the Internet. Bruno Bonnell, managing director of Infogrammes, believes that by 2002 online games will account for 20 per cent of their turnover. Nevertheless the CD-Rom industry does not seem to feel threatened with extinction.

Different types of game

• Classic games such as Chess and Go.
• Role playing games such as Diablo 2.
• War games such as Command & Conquer.
• 3D Labyrinth games such as Doom or Quake, where the virtual environment consists of a series of rooms and corridors where horrible opponents are lurking. In many ways these are the graphical descendants of the classic MUDs (Multi User Dungeons), especially as they can now be played over networks.
• Growth games such as Civilization or SimCity, where the player builds and develops a nation or a city.

e-commerce

There is no need to go out in the rain and queue for the bus, you can wander around the virtual high street on a Saturday afternoon in the comfort of your own home and buy just about everything on the Net.

True globalisation

Whatever you buy the procedure is the same. Choose your product, enter your card number, give your name and address and that's it. Generally you will receive a confirmatory e-mail from the supplier and the goods will be posted to you a few days later. However, it is not just goods that you can now buy over the Internet, the financial sector is aiming to scoop up lots of cyber consumers too, and is eager to sell mortgages, insurance, and set up online bank accounts. The expenditure necessary for online selling is minimal, but logistics, marketing and computer systems create much higher costs than is the case with commercial set-ups. This is why profit margins are still poor in e-commerce and progress in this area depends primarily upon numbers visiting the sites in question.

CONSUMER RIGHTS

In the UK the consumer has the same rights regarding items bought over the Net as for those bought in conventional outlets. The goods should be as described on the Web site, of satisfactory quality and be fit for their purpose. For more information visit the Office of Fair Trading's site at www.oft.gov.uk. However, this safety net does not apply if buying something from abroad, when the consumer is subject to other country's laws. It is likely also to be harder to return or exchange goods bought from foreign sites.

Secure payment on the Internet

The first question the prospective Internet shopper asks is, can my credit card number be stolen? The answer is yes, but the dangers are really no greater than when you use it in the conventional way. Encryption systems cannot guarantee 100 per cent protection, but they do mean that as soon as you enter a secure site, and nearly all shopping sites will be secure (see box, left), your card number is, contrary to popular belief, pretty safe. Even more secure systems such as Secure Electronic Transactions (SET) are beginning to come into usage. Furthermore, in many countries your bank will generally cover you for fraudulent usage of your card.

Useful online shopping precautions

• Check that the Web site has a full physical address (not just a PO box number) and telephone number. Phone the number and see who answers.
• Check that the site is secure – the address should begin with https://. The 's' means the site is secure and that it is using an encryption system that makes it possible to ensure the confidentiality of transactions. In addition, look for a security symbol on the top left of your browser screen, a blue key in Explorer and a padlock in Netscape Communicator.
• Visit sites where consumers rate the site and give opinions on their shopping experiences there (www.bizrate.com).
• Keep proof of your order, eg. a print-out of your order.
• Check the terms of the site's returns or goodwill policy and look for a site's privacy policy in which it should undertake to keep information confidential and not to pass it on to a third party.
• Never reveal your PIN code to anyone.
• Look for sites displaying a trading standards logo where sites should undertake to comply with a commercial code of good practice, though this is not a guarantee that the site will comply with the code.

99 £

TOTAL 171 £

Internet users – who are you?

According to recent statistics Internet use in the UK is fairly evenly divided between men and women aged 15–54, which is surprising for those who consider the Internet to be rather a 'techy' male dominated area. Men aged 15–24 represent nearly 10% and women 7.5% of all users, though more women aged 25–34 (10.5%) than men (6%) are currently using the Net. As you may expect, children account for a large proportion of users – over 17% of those aged 2–14 go online. During the first quarter of 2001 the average age of Internet users rose, with a surge of over-55s using the Net to book their holidays and manage their finances.

TRACKING AND PROFILING
Analyse the sites a user consults to build up a consumer profile.

What do you use the Internet for?

E-mail is the most common Internet activity – 97 per cent of those who log on use it. 84 per cent claim that they use the Net to look for information on specific subjects. 75 per cent of users download software, or find out about a product or service (73 per cent).

Online commerce is gaining in popularity. 45 per cent of UK net users have already made at least one online purchase. Cultural interests are well represented on the shopping list, books and music, for example, make up a large proportion of all online sales.

GETTING TO KNOW YOU – INTERNET PROFILING

Cookies are small text files that, unknown to the user, are planted on his or her hard disk by the Web site when the user visits it. In this way sites are able to track a user's habits and build up a customer profile. This information can then potentially be passed on to companies that want to sell their products, resulting in the user receiving unsolicited advertising. Cookies do therefore smack of 'Big Brother', but they can be examined and disabled with software such as Cookie Crusher (www.thelimitsoft.com), IDcide Privacy Companion (www.idcide.com), or many other freeware and shareware programmes downloadable from the Internet. Cookies also have a beneficial side as they can be used to remember your personal details (useful when logging back into a frequently visited site), or to keep track of an online ordering session.

Is the Internet divisive?

Internet access is partly limited by the cost of buying the necessary equipment, and partly by a tendency for it to be used in a working context, in particular by office workers who represent 50 per cent of Internet users, as opposed to the 17 per cent of manual/unskilled workers and employees who use the Internet.

However, provision of IT centres is on the increase, and retail prices are falling, so that access to the Web will hopefully become more widespread. Some shops and businesses have installed computers in their premises for their customers to access the Internet, and Internet cafés are becoming more commonplace.

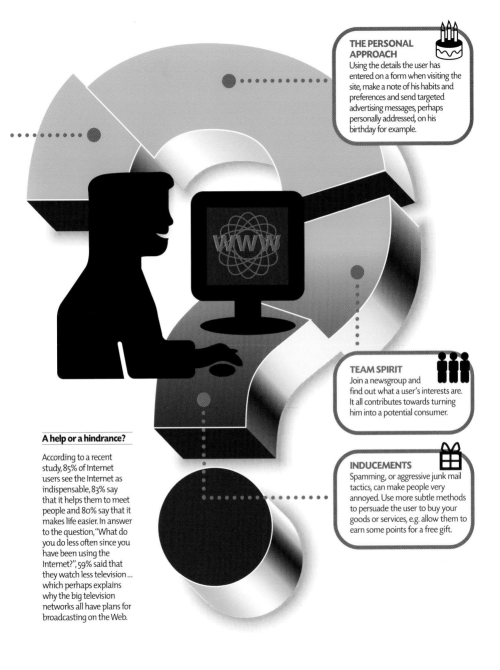

THE PERSONAL APPROACH

Using the details the user has entered on a form when visiting the site, make a note of his habits and preferences and send targeted advertising messages, perhaps personally addressed, on his birthday for example.

TEAM SPIRIT

Join a newsgroup and find out what a user's interests are. It all contributes towards turning him into a potential consumer.

INDUCEMENTS

Spamming, or aggressive junk mail tactics, can make people very annoyed. Use more subtle methods to persuade the user to buy your goods or services, e.g. allow them to earn some points for a free gift.

A help or a hindrance?

According to a recent study, 85% of Internet users see the Internet as indispensable, 83% say that it helps them to meet people and 80% say that it makes life easier. In answer to the question, "What do you do less often since you have been using the Internet?", 59% said that they watch less television ... which perhaps explains why the big television networks all have plans for broadcasting on the Web.

Cybercriminals

Crime has unfortunately kept pace with Internet growth and the Web is vulnerable from various angles, ranging from the theft of a graphic image, a game or a piece of music, to whole sites being wiped out.

HACKERS
Hackers are usually idealists who would like to restore the early freedom and altruistic aims that surrounded the creation of the Internet, to demonstrate the fragility of the system, or simply to be noticed. Their attacks target big commercial sites or organisations that try or claim to control the network. The hacker may briefly bring the site down.

Real criminals

At this level we are no longer talking about simply raiding a card number. For a long time now criminals have been able to give themselves false identities. But illegal acts do not stop there. Cyber criminals are active in all walks of life, and often on a corporate level. They may be disgruntled employees who steal or destroy company information, bogus traders who generate fake publicity for shares in an unsuspecting company, which they then sell at a handsome profit, or cyber-terrorists who hack into high-profile Websites to add a political message or hold large organisations to ransom with the threat of crashing their servers.
Probably the most infamous corporate hacking case is still that of Timothy Lloyd, a former network administrator for Omega Engineering Corp, a large company listing NASA and the US Navy among its customers. Lloyd had fallen from favour in the company, and was eventually fired in 1996, but not before he had programmed a computer time-bomb to wipe out everything on the company's main servers. On the morning of July 31st, 1996, Omega lost software, programmes and data which wound up costing the company $10m, and irreversibly dislodged its footing in the industry. Although it took four years, investigators eventually managed to convict Lloyd and bring him to trial. He was convicted in May 2000.

CRACKERS
Driven by a real desire to do harm, the targets might be the same as those of hackers, but their motives are quite different. They are out to destroy, steal secure data and infiltrate systems, often looking for financial gain.

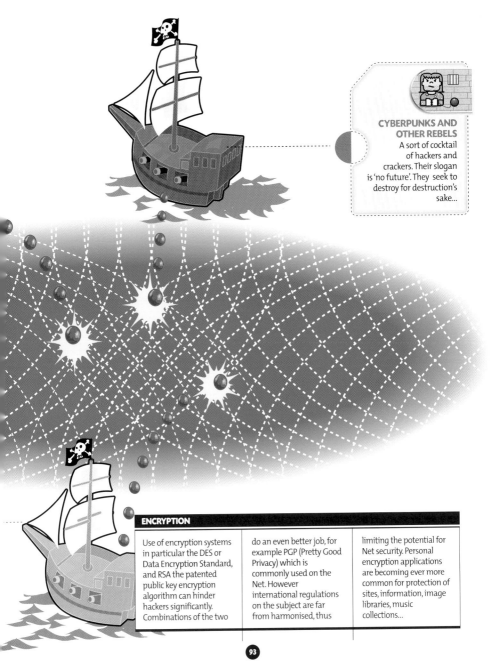

ENCRYPTION

Use of encryption systems in particular the DES or Data Encryption Standard, and RSA the patented public key encryption algorithm can hinder hackers significantly. Combinations of the two do an even better job, for example PGP (Pretty Good Privacy) which is commonly used on the Net. However international regulations on the subject are far from harmonised, thus limiting the potential for Net security. Personal encryption applications are becoming ever more common for protection of sites, information, image libraries, music collections...

Creating your own site

As people cruise around the Internet they begin to discover home-grown sites and sooner or later many feel the urge to stamp their own mark on the Web. The forbidding technological barrier that once surrounded the Net has now been broken down and today everyone can be a part of it if they so wish. All you need is something that you want to communicate to people, a little time, and a basic understanding of HTML and Java. Service providers often provide free Web space for a modestly sized site in their subscription package. 10 MB of space is the norm, but for a reasonable sum you could be granted more.

SUGGESTIONS TO GET STARTED

- Make a plan of the site.
- Write the text.
- Choose the artwork.
- Settle on a graphic chart.
- Create the pages using appropriate software (html, java …).
- Take care over the home page, navigation tools, the visitor interface.
- Test out the site with friends.
- Load the pages onto an Internet Service Provider's Web server.
- Publicise the site.
- Keep your site fresh and update information regularly.

- NB: Care should taken when using images, sound or anything else originating from the Web. Most material on the Web is copyrighted by someone, and you should gain permission from the copyright holder if you intend to use their work on your own site.

WEB PAGE EDITORS

Web page editors are the equivalent of word processing packages for Websites. They enable you to easily create and edit pages, without having to understand the underlying HTML code.

They range from basic packages (such as FrontPage Express) to enterprise level products which are used by industry professionals. (Macromedia Dreamweaver and FrontPage 2000).

FrontPage Express is a basic WYSIWYG (what you see is what you get) Web page editor that is supplied free with Windows 98. It can also be downloaded from the Microsoft Website (www.microsoft.com).

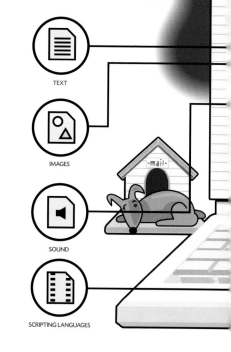

TEXT

IMAGES

SOUND

SCRIPTING LANGUAGES

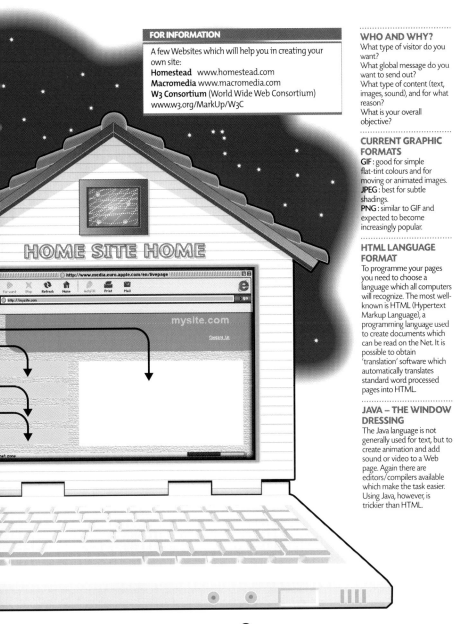

HOME SITE HOME

http://www.media.euro.apple.com/en/livepage

http://mysite.com

mysite.com

Contact Us

WHO AND WHY?

What type of visitor do you want? What global message do you want to send out? What type of content (text, images, sound), and for what reason? What is your overall objective?

CURRENT GRAPHIC FORMATS

GIF : good for simple flat-tint colours and for moving or animated images. **JPEG** : best for subtle shadings. **PNG** : similar to GIF and expected to become increasingly popular.

HTML LANGUAGE FORMAT

To programme your pages you need to choose a language which all computers will recognize. The most well-known is HTML (Hypertext Markup Language), a programming language used to create documents which can be read on the Net. It is possible to obtain 'translation' software which automatically translates standard word processed pages into HTML.

JAVA – THE WINDOW DRESSING

The Java language is not generally used for text, but to create animation and add sound or video to a Web page. Again there are editors/compilers available which make the task easier. Using Java, however, is trickier than HTML.

Images and the Internet

Animated or still, there are images everywhere on the Internet. Graphics, pictures and animation have become part of the Web's character, adding interest to sites and making them fun to visit.

Digital images

If you want to include an image on your Web site you can obtain one from an online photo library, as suggested by the big directories. For more personal visuals your first step is the process of digitisation. Personal photos can be digitised using a scanner, or else created with a digital camera. For video digitisation use analogue tape software, or a digital camcorder. In the first case you put your photo on the scanner platen. The photo is then scanned and transformed into a grid of coloured dots known as a pixel image (pixel: a contraction of 'picture element'). With video, software performs the same task. You can produce perfectly good pictures on the Internet without having to use high definition scanning or photography. Computer screens vary from a basic 640 x 480 pixels to very high resolutions of 1,280 x 1,024 pixels.

Web cams

Web cams are small cameras for computers. They are used for video-conferencing or to record images to include in Web pages, messages etc. Low prices but high entertainment value make them a 'best seller' among computer peripherals. Internet users install Web cams which continually record one spot, an apartment, a hamster's cage or the corner shop and the images are sent out directly on the Internet. However, don't expect to see continuous action as on the television or in a film – in general the images are stills that are updated every 30 seconds.

WHERE DO INTERNET IMAGES COME FROM?

- ▢ **TELEVISION**
- ⊡ **SCANNING**
- ▦ **DIGITAL PHOTO**
- ◉ **CD**
- ✦ **WEBCAM**
- ▧ **ONLINE IMAGE LIBRARY**

Television on the Net

It is possible to pick up television over the Internet. However, it is worth noting that if you want to view an animated image and sound at the same time, you must have a high speed telephone line (ISDN or ADSL).
These days all the big television companies are considering putting their programmes on the Net, but so far there is little to see. To receive programmes properly you need a high speed line and a suitable modem, which entails more expense than a standard television set.

Webcam madness

Webcams can be amusing. Use these directories to help you unearth a few good addresses and sites. But watch out – the Webcam world is always on the move and addresses can quickly change.

DIRECTORIES
www.annucam.com
Over 500 Webcams divided into categories
www.webcamsearch.com
A 'must' for well-informed 'Webcammers'. With 11,000 sites referenced this directory is the biggest and most comprehensive.

Netmeetings

This is chat (p.99) with sound and vision. If the participants have Web cams, they can film themselves and send out the images, while conversing via the keyboard. With the right equipment sound can also play a part.

However, even with high speed connections, the visual effect is more like a sequence of stills rather than a continuous film. A one-to-one dialogue with images and sound is possible.

TRY THESE WEB CAM SITES		
www.ispy.com/ webcams Keep watch over the entrance to a French bakery and see people emerging with, croissants, baguettes and other goodies.	**www.kremlinkam.com** The Kremlin in Moscow. If you are lucky you might spot Vladimir Putin. **www.isracamera.co.il** Dolphins in an	aquarium, filmed using an underwater camera. **www.lochness.co.uk** Keep an eye on Loch Ness. You might see the monster!

WAP: have Internet, will travel

WAP stands for 'Wireless Applications Protocol'. Behind the acronym lurks a system that lets you access the Internet through a GSM telephone. With WAP you can explore the Web from your mobile telephone, pick up your e-mails anywhere and at any time.

The mobile Internet

It seems strange to be able to access the Web with a phone! A mobile only has a small, black and white screen, and data transmission speeds are low (9,600 bps). So in fact you don't exactly 'surf' the Net – at a pinch you might be able to look at your e-mail, or send one, if it's not too long. Nothing particularly exciting – however, it is likely that GSM will become linked to specific services and that there will also be a significant increase in speed thanks to GPRS (see below). It will not be long before GSM phones come with an integral credit card payment terminal. Bigger, colour screens will be available at reasonable prices so today's WAP terminals might be the mobile multimedia terminals of tomorrow.

WAP abroad

Japan provides the most advanced example of this new technology. In the Land of the Rising Sun they do not use WAP, but a system known as I-mode which is designed to run on the Japanese NTT network. Since its introduction about 18 months ago, I-mode has met with great success, and now has over 7,000,000 customers and several thousand sites, though it has not yet been adopted anywhere else in the world. Although I-mode is a proprietary technology (specific to the Japanese company DoCoMo), it is simpler to implement and use than WAP. DoCoMo are looking at introducing a European version which will run on the GPRS network (See below). This is already being seen as a potential challenge to the WAP standard. In Italy, Omnitel 2000 already offers around 150 different services and in Germany, D2 is currently venturing into the market. In Sweden WAP took off early in the year 2000. In the United States, the operator Sprint has introduced a mobile data service using WAP, in partnership with Yahoo! as the portal. Sites and services on offer can only increase.

GPRS

GPRS stands for 'General Packet Radio Service'. It is a new data transmission standard for mobiles, which should, initially, give speeds of 64 kbps, later to be doubled. Amongst other things, GPRS will make it possible for information to be sent, not just to one subscriber, but to a group of subscribers. The operators will have to make a significant investment in order to get their networks up to scratch, but this technology (which will also allow transmission of images to mobiles) should quite quickly become less expensive. It will also pave the way for I-mode to infiltrate the European Market (see above).

RACES

BANKING

TOURISM

STOCK MARKET

INTERNET

SHOPPING

ADDRESS BOOK

WEATHER

Info
weather
address book
e-mail
games

Chat rooms and newsgroups

ICQ (I SEEK YOU)

ICQ lets you talk in real-time, privately among friends or just with one person. It can function offline and allows you to know who is connected. Each new user is given a personal number and is asked various questions. He or she will then appear in a visible directory of addresses. An audio signal indicates when a contact is made. A disadvantage is that you need additional software as, you don't use a Web browser.

The Web makes it easy to form relationships with strangers. Chat rooms create fleeting contact with other people, or sometimes much more. Ten per cent of Internet users meet up in real life, having first conversed in the virtual world.

On the other side of the world ...

Chat is conversation live, in real-time via text messages – an ideal means of communicating with someone the other side of the world for just the price of a local telephone call. You can chat with friends or join a newsgroup, a discussion group devoted to a certain subject. It is estimated there are about 23,000 newsgroups in the world. The most famous system is called Usenet which sub-divides topics into smaller categories. You post a message to the group and anyone who subscribes to that group can reply. Newsgroups represent a useful way of obtaining an answer to specific questions, compared with search engines which can cast their Net too widely and indiscriminately. Post your question to the relevant interest group and you are likely to receive several answers within the space of a few hours from people who have a good knowledge of the subject.

IRC (Internet Relay Chat)

Conversations are live, as with ICQ, but the difference is that it is like opening the door of a room, not knowing who you will find in there. When you type in a message, it will immediately be transmitted to everybody who is in the same channel. The software can be a bit tricky to use, difficult for beginners. You give yourself a nickname, select a server and join a channel.

FAQS (FREQUENTLY ASKED QUESTIONS)

FAQs are lists of questions posted at regular intervals to newsgroups for the benefit of new subscribers. They contain the most common questions and answers posted to that group. Newcomers are therefore strongly recommended to read the list of FAQs when they join, in order to avoid the embarrassment of posting a potentially repetitive question which would be tedious for regular users.

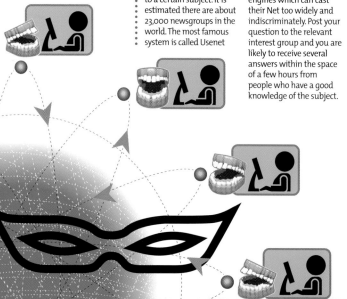

FIND OUT

WHO ARE THE MOVERS AND SHAKERS OF THE NET?

WOULD YOU LIKE TO JOIN THEM?

JOB OPPORTUNITIES ON THE WEB.

SUGGESTIONS FOR A BASIC SOFTWARE LIBRARY.

A SELECTION OF INTERNET SITES TO GET YOU STARTED.

USEFUL ADDRESSES TO FIND OUT MORE.

Masters of the Net Universe

Who are the movers and shakers of the brave new world of the Internet? Here are some of the visionary individuals who got the whole thing going and whose companies are today worth millions.

Bill Gates, the richest man in the world

Crazy about computers and gifted with exceptional business sense, Bill Gates is the founder of Microsoft and Internet Explorer. Some regard him as a genius, but once the darling of the Net and the world of micro-computing, his reputation has now become tarnished as others denigrate his increasing wealth. At the end of 1999 he handed over the reins at Microsoft to his right hand man Steve Ballmer. Microsoft had been heavily criticised – the company was accused of not giving users protection against cookies, the computer 'spies' that track users' Web navigation habits and it was also accused of having too much power. Microsoft is currently under the threat of being broken up, a threat which has in part already been carried out.

Steve Case, Managing Director of AOL (America Online)

The son of a commercial lawyer and a primary school teacher, Steve Case has kept his youthful looks and cultivates a jeans and trainers image. As a sixth former he managed a small fruit juice business. Later he worked in marketing for Proctor & Gamble and Pizza Hut, before starting up a small video game company, Control Video Co. which would later grow to become America Online. The trigger came in 1983 when Case was using his computer to gain access to something resembling an online service, and realised the Internet's enormous potential. He took the rungs of the ladder two at a time and today heads up a business empire which boasts over 22 million subscribers.

At the end of 1999/early 2000, the AOL lion roared loudly indeed – the company acquired Time Warner, the leading communications, press and cinema company, thus becoming owner of *Time* magazine, Warner Bros Studios and the television channels CNN and HBO. A few weeks later it swallowed up EMI, the music-publishing house. At the time, the press had been following the stories closely but had not even mentioned AOL as a possible candidate to buy out these two giants. There was much surprise despite the fact that AOL had already demonstrated its muscle by buying out Compuserve, ICQ and Netscape.

Ted Turner, Vice Chairman of Time Warner

This energetic leading light of the media is conspicuous for his union with AOL. He established Turner Broadcasting System (TBS) which was at the forefront of the cable industry in the 1970s. In the 1980s he established Cable News Network (CNN) and Turner Network Television (TNT). Turner then bought MGM/United Artists Entertainment Company, but was forced to sell MGM in order to retain control of TBS which Turner then sold on to Time Warner in 1995, where he became Vice Chairman. At one time married to Jane Fonda, Turner has spent a long time in the public eye, but surprised everyone in 1997 when he donated $1 billion to the United Nations. Now well over sixty, with neat moustache and silver hair, his has been the classic American success story and now he is moving over to the new technology. Watch this space for further mega bucks moves!

Jeff Bezos, founder of Amazon.com

Books were not doing so well. They had lost their appeal. So why not give them a bright new look by putting them online? It was this gamble which led Jeff Bezos to create Amazon.com. This much visited site typifies businesses where market value is based on subscriber numbers, rather than on real economic clout. Selling a vast range of DVDs, videos and music as well as books, Amazon.com has in fact yet to make a profit, a clear example of the enormous cost and difficulty of starting up a successful business online. Bezos, a gifted communicator, has been nominated personality of the year by *Time* magazine.

Tim Koogle, boss of Yahoo!

'When we have identified a strategic acquisition, we do not look at how many dollars we have to spend. Rather we assess whether the impact of buying the shares will be compensated for by that company's future contribution to our profit,' explained Tim Koogle, Managing Director of Yahoo! (Taken from an article by Dominique Nora in *Nouvel Observateur* 13-19 May 1999). Tim Koogle is an opportunist; ready to seize the opportunity for the next profitable merger. Yahoo! is one of the most well-known and best of the general directories that has grown rapidly with sites all over the world. By mid-1999 the UK site was receiving over three million visits a week It is one of the biggest successes in terms of turnover, profits and stockmarket value of the Net economy.

The Internet at the cinema

Not surprisingly Hollywood scriptwriters have turned their attention to the Internet. However it was not until 1995 that the Web became the backdrop to a box-office hit.

The Net

An American film directed in 1995 by Irwin Winkler, with Sandra Bullock, Jeremy Northam and Dennis Miller. *The Net* is a real thriller of the kind at which American movie-makers excel. It is the story of a young computer analyst (Angela) who works from her home in Los Angeles for a software company based in San Francisco. Her job involves tracing viruses and giving telephone advice to customers. She also spends a fair amount of her leisure time on the Net participating in newsgroups on computing. Somebody sends her a suspect programme and tells her that he will visit the next day to discuss it with her. However his aeroplane crashes and it is this accident which triggers the action-packed story. The programme in question attracts the interest of some criminals who will stop at nothing to get hold of it. They make the heroine 'vanish' from computer records (no ID papers, no car, no credit cards) and then attempt to kill her. A gripping film that met with well-deserved success and led to a long-running television series.

Johnny Mnemonic

Johnny Mnemonic, directed by Robert Longu, with Keanu Reeves, Dolph Lundgren and Takeshi Kitano, also came out in 1995, though the Internet features rather more anecdotally in the film than in *The Net*. 'Fantasy' might best describe it in terms of genre. Johnny is a young man living in the year 2021. Multi-national companies rule the world, and a fatal illness (Nervous Atrophy Syndrome), caused by excessive bombardment of information, is decimating the population. A resistance group is formed which communicates using 'mnemonic couriers', individuals who have had data implanted in their brains. One of the effects of this operation is that childhood memories are wiped out. Johnny is one of these couriers, given the job of transporting a formula containing a cure for the fatal syndrome. One of the multi-nationals had wanted to keep the formula secret in order to continue to profit from the epidemic. Having triumphed over numerous adversaries, Johnny finally delivers the precious formula that will help save humanity. He also gets back his childhood memories.

You've Got Mail

A romantic comedy directed by Nora Ephron in 1998, starring Tom Hanks, Meg Ryan and Parker Posey, where the Internet plays a big part in the action. The film begins with the two main characters clashing. Joe Fox, heir to an influential bookselling business, is about to open a giant bookstore in a district of New York. Just next door Kathleen Kelly has a lovely little shop selling children's books, which her mother opened forty years previously, 'The Shop around the Corner'. The two protagonists, who know each other very well under the names 'NY152' and 'Shopgirl' which they use on Internet newsgroups, are completely unaware of their respective virtual identities. Their meeting in the real world leads to a string of misunderstandings and developments ... and to a love story, naturally. The film conveys well the appeal of e-mail, chat rooms and newsgroups.

Tron

This film was one of the first of the modern fantasy genre. Directed by Steven Lisberger in 1982 and made by Walt Disney Productions, *Tron* is the story of a researcher who, reduced to microscopic size, finds himself trapped in the circuits of a computer. Cartoon artist Moebius (alias Jean Giraud) was involved in the artistic design of the film which was pretty revolutionary for the time. The Internet features in the film, but does not have a starring role.

Online careers

Artistic director

It is his or her job to make the site attractive and to make sure that navigation through the site is intuitive.

Consultant

Analyses the market, looks for novel ideas, advises on multimedia products or services and future directions.

Developer

Develops software applications and scripting for Web platforms.

Flash animator

Flash is increasingly being used to liven up Web pages. Graphically-minded, technically confident animators are in demand to increase the visibility of companies' brands.

Game designer

Works with graphic designers and programmers on designing and developing video games.

Graphic designer/Designer

Creates or edits the graphical elements of a site, which may include company logos, retouched photographs, navigation buttons, backgrounds and animations.

Production editor

Must delegate the editorial workload and make sure the talents of the editorial staff are being put to best use. Some writing and editing is usually involved. Should usually be educated to degree level and be an excellent communicator

Project manager

The project manager is in overall charge of a project and collaborates with graphic designers, marketing people and editors.

Sales manager

Develops the sales strategy and manages and motivates the sales team. Must be driven by the desire to make a profit, as the bottom line is all-important.

Web designer

Is involved in site design and presentation. Must know about standard software and programming languages.

Web marketer

Develops tools to measure how often the site is visited.

Webmaster

Takes overall charge of the administration of a site, managing it and keeping it up-to-date.

Hot-liner

The hot-liner gives advice to Internet users on behalf of an Internet Service Provider. Often self-taught.

Moderator

In Usenet and mailing lists, the moderator screens messages received, generally guides visitors and provokes discussion.

Netsurfer

Monitors the Net, compares sites and reports back to the service provider.

Online advertising manager

Sells advertising space for Websites.

Online editor

Has to manage editorial content. Must know the limitations of a Website, but must also be able to exploit its possibilities.

Online journalist

Writes up articles in collaboration with the Web editor. Generally does not have the right to a press card.

Training courses

There are a huge range of courses focused on both career development and personal interest. Find out more by visiting these URLs and see what is on offer.

Courses are run by local Colleges of Further Education at a local level, or university degrees at the national level; these concentrate on major subjects such as computer engineering and programming, business studies and management.

www.hobsons.com provide a central resource to find out who does what. The same is true of **http://uk.dir.yahoo.com/regional/Countries/ UnitedKingdom/Education/HigherEducation/ Colleges and Universities/** (note the lack of 'www' – this is increasingly common as the Web develops).

If you want more targeted training such as how to learn to use a specific piece of software, look at independent training companies offering courses ranging from one day to several weeks. Companies regularly send their key staff along for training.

www.ariseeducation.com (don't forget to download their free 'world time' screensaver!)

And as you would expect, there are also plenty of online educational resources and training facilities, as well as vast quantities of general information that will help you build up an overall picture.

www.netskills.ac.uk

Based at the University of Newcastle, Netskills provides three kinds of service: workshops and on-site training around the country, providing teaching materials for other Internet teachers, and TONIC, the online introduction to the Internet that you can follow at your own pace.

www.hairnet.org

Especially for those who haven't grown up with the Internet. For a fee of £20 an hour plus expenses they provide home tuition; they also cater for the corporate and voluntary sectors, offering training and lectures.

UNIVERSITIES AND COLLEGES ADMISSIONS SERVICE

www.ucas.co.uk

Gives comprehensive listings of higher education courses in the UK, mainly aimed at the prospective undergraduate. Includes breakdowns of courses with names of the modules and components, contact details and information on campus layout and the provision of accommodation. Lists 144 Internet courses, including Internet Marketing, Computer Games and Internet Technology, Internet Law and Society, at institutions around the country.

www.hotcourses.com

A very large database (lists around 150,000 courses), freely accessible on the web. Here you will find evening and weekend courses that can be combined with a job or other activity. Lists 24 Internet courses (eg. Web Page Design, Introduction to the Internet, Web Publishing) that take place at weekends.

OPEN UNIVERSITY

www.open.ac.uk

Offers a diploma and three bachelor's degrees in Information Technology. Its courses range from 'You, Your Computer and the Net' to 'Artificial Intelligence for Technology', and take place largely online. Course fees are £100–£200 for UK residents.

DEPARTMENT FOR EDUCATION AND EMPLOYMENT

www.dfee.gov.uk

The British government department overseeing work and training. It covers everything from primary schools to getting a job; the Website includes useful information for those returning to education after a period at work or who want to learn specific skills, including information technology and Web skills, in order to improve their job prospects.

UK ONLINE

An organization that, with the support of a broad base of government and industry groups, aims to increase the percentage of the UK population that has access to the Internet, and encourage the country's sapling knowledge economy.
Tel: 0114 2593226
ukonlinecentres@dfee.gov.uk

CITY UNIVERSITY

www.city.ac.uk

City University, in the heart of London, has been a leader in the teaching and researching of information science ever since it introduced its course on 'Collecting and Communicating Scientific Knowledge' in 1961. Its postgraduate courses include an MSc in Information Systems and Technology, and another in Electronic Publishing.

www.free-ed.net

Based in Ohio, USA, free-ed.net offers free online education, but does not give out diplomas or certificates (it is designed to complement, not replace, school-based courses). There are so many IT courses on offer they take up a whole separate catalogue. Provides instruction in computer languages such as HTML and Java as well as a full course of lessons in 'Using the Internet'.

www.symmedia.co.uk

An independent training centre that offers courses in Web design and marketing, and will help you master the arts of HTML, Flash, Dreamweaver, Frontpage and other Web-related packages.

Useful sites

There are millions to choose from. Here is a tiny selection, just the very tip of the iceberg, to get you started.

Group purchases

Consumer groups combine to offer better prices through bulk purchasing:
www.which.net has one of the best known sites for general consumer goods, or
www.egroups.co.uk/dir/Shopping provides a portal from which you can find a shopping group that interests you – there are hundreds!
www.letsbuyit.com/en_GB a Swedish group represented in 14 countries.
www.mobshop.co.uk specialises in computer hardware, electronics and PDAs, small hand-held computers.
www.uniondream.com/GB_ is represented in several European countries and offers a large assortment of products and brands.

Auctions

Sell the contents of your loft or buy someone else's:
www.ebay.co.uk
www.qxl.co.uk
www.onlineauctions.co.uk

Supermarkets

www.tesco.com for home deliveries of food.
www.iceland.co.uk specialising in frozen food but also in organics.
www.sainsburys.co.uk
www.waitrose.com

Travel and tourism

www.lastminute.com for that spur of the moment decision to take off – includes many other recreational offers.

www.thomascook.com for an armchair browse through the holidays on offer.

www.waterbynature.com if you just can't resist whitewater rafting.

Employment

Many of the big agencies have their own sites, and offer a service that finds a job to suit you rather than just offering you a list to browse. **www.reed.co.uk** is one such. List sites include:
www.jobwatch.co.uk
www.monster.co.uk
www.jobworlduk.co.uk

Estate Agents

www.homes-on-line.com
www.studio5.co.uk/beag/default.html houses the British Estate Agents Group site.
www.countrylife.co.uk
www.oea.org is the Ombudsman's site – useful when things go awry.

Stock Exchange

www.ft.com for the Financial Times.
www.charles-schwab.com
www.swifttrade.com

Newspapers and magazines

www.the-times.co.uk
www.telegraph.co.uk
www.independent.co.uk
www.guardianunlimited.co.uk
www.dailymail.co.uk
www.mirror.co.uk
www.newsdirectory.com/news/magazine/eu/uk/ for a portal on magazines.

TV and radio

www.bbc.co.uk
www.classicfm.co.uk
www.carlton.com
www.itc.org.uk
www.channel4.co.uk

Books

www.amazon.co.uk
www.waterstones.co.uk
www.blackwell.co.uk for professional and academic books.
www.ottakars.co.uk
www.uk.bol.com
www.whsmith.co.uk

net.co.uk/fores

http://www.tele.net/

http://www.zambesi.org

Useful sites

Music

www.amazon.co.uk
www.abbeyrecords.com if you're into vinyl!
www.virginmega.com
www.sonymusic.co.uk
www.cd-wow.co.uk
www.101cd.com

Online Games

www.gamesdomain.com has a good selection.
www.jamba.co.uk
www.igl.net for *Quake* and other league games.
http://www.zone.com
www.games.yahoo.com

Children

www.kidsdomain.co.uk
www.thomasthetankengine.com
www.seaworld.org
www.insect-world.com
www.nationalgeographic.com/kids
www.yahooligans.com for 8–14 year olds.
www.funmail.com
www.popworld.com
www.bbc.co.uk/kids

Bartering

www.barter.co.uk
www.ebay.co.uk
www.bartercard.com
www.zdnet.co.uk
www.bartertrust.com
www.homexchange.com if you're thinking of travelling and want to barter space in your home for space in someone else's home.
www.swap.shop.com mostly for guitars, but some other miscellaneous items.
www.ugtz.com (Used Game Trading Zone) allows computer and video game owners to trade games they no longer play for games they would like to play.

Art

www.tate.org.uk for the UK's best-known gallery.
www.nationalgallery.org.uk
www.npg.org.uk for the National Portrait Gallery.
www.ica.org.uk to find out about the Institute of Contemporary Arts.
www.hayward-gallery.org.uk
www.royalacademy.org.uk
www.The-Wallace-Collection.org.uk
www.prints.worc.ox.ac.uk to find out about the George Clarke Print collection.
www.gainsborough.org
www.fitzmuseum.cam.ac.uk for the Fitzwilliam Museum.
www.dulwichpicturegallery.org.uk
www.daliuniverse.com for information about Salvador Dali.

Learning to drive

www.driving.co.uk will help you with the test
www.driving-schools.co.uk can help you find the ideal instructor.
www.learners.co.uk
www.learning2drive.co.uk

www.bsm.co.uk (British School of Motoring)
www.britannia-driving-school.co.uk
www.highwaymotoring.demon.co.uk

MP3

www.peoplesound.com for MP3 music files to hear and download. They sign up artists who want to spread their music through the Web, and you can buy files online that you like. Multilingual site. You can also download an MP3 player if you do not already have one.

There are many other music Websites, catering for all types of music:
www.britishclassicalmusic.com
www.musicweb.uk.net
www.classicalmusic.co.uk
www.royalopera.org
www.glyndebourne.com
www.scottishopera.org.uk
www.goh.co.uk (Grand Opera House, Belfast)
www.wno.org.uk (Welsh National Opera)
www.musicnet.com
www.emusic.com
www.playlouder.co.uk
www.icrunch.co.uk

Are you ready to surf the Net?

Now try out your knowledge. Take our 'surfing' test and see what your chances are of finding your way around the Web.

1 • WWW (World Wide Web) is the name:

a - Of the entire Internet
b - Of a part of the Internet
c - Of an Internet Service Provider

2 • MP3 means:

a - Music Player 3
b - MPEG3
c - Magical Phono 3

3 • The iloveyou virus, transmitted on the Internet, affected:

a - PC compatibles
b - Macs
c - PC compatibles and Macs

4 • Search engines are used to:

a - Speed up your computer
b - Find a site
c - Travel more quickly around the Net

5 • WAP technology allows you to:

a - Access the Internet from a mobile telephone
b - Listen to hits from the sixties
c - Look for a particular site

6 • Java is:

a - A computer programme
b - A Web festival
c - A programming language

7 • 'Chats' on the Internet are:

a - Unobtainable sites on the Internet
b - Discussion groups
c - Difficult routes on the Web

8 • An ISP is:

a - A company which provides access to the Internet
b - A site specialising in the stock market
c - A site manager

9 • A hacker is:

a - A virus
b - A computer pirate
c - A piece of hardware used in Internet telephony

10 • Vinton Cerf is:

a - An antivirus programme
b - One of the founders of Microsoft
c - One of the inventors of the Internet

11 • SoHo is:

a - A 'red light' district in London
b - An abbreviation of Small Office Home Office
c - A new technique for transmitting data

12 • e-commerce relates to:

a - Selling electricity
b - Trade on the Internet
c - The commercialisation of emails

13 • Internet linking of the first two computers (at the Universities of Los Angeles and Stanford) took place in:

a - 1959
b - 1969
c - 1979

Answers: 1/b.2/b.3/a.4/b.5/a.6/c.7/b.
8/a.9/b.10/c.11/b.12/b.13/b

Do you speak Net?

Here is a short glossary of 'net language'. The rest is up to the Internet user's imagination . . .

Smileys

:-) I'm smiling

:-(I'm sad

»:-» I'm mischievous

»;-» I'm in the mood for love!

#-) I had a great time last night

%-(I) I'm doubled up with laughing

:-$ I'm ill

:'-(I'm crying

:) I'm happy

:-# Mum's the word

Father Christmas

:-' I'm a smoker

:-X A very big kiss

( ) No comment

:-0 I'm shouting

:----) You're a liar

P-(Pirate

ACHTUNG! CIAO! PARLEZ-VOUS?

Many software packages, usually in English, tend to misinterpret the accents used in foreign languages. This is very noticeable when it comes to e-mails, addresses and user names. To avoid sending indecipherable messages in a foreign language, the only solution is to give up using accents. However, watch out for potential ambiguities and wrong meanings.

English, a universal language

AFK: away from keyboard
BBN: bye bye now
BRB: be right back
BWL: bursting with laughter
CU (or 6U): see you
F2F: face to face (used to describe a real world meeting).
4U: for you
H2H: head to head or a personal message
HAGN: have a good night
HHOJ: HaHa only joking
IM: individual message
INTRW: in the real world
L8R: later
LOL: laughing out loud
MORF: male or female?
PTMM: please tell me more
ROFL: rolling on the floor laughing loudly
Room: a virtual place where Internet users meet to chat
S3M: scream
TNX: thanks
U2: you too
Yo: rap expression, widely used as you enter a room

I'm shocked!

I'm winking

I'm really depressed

Not a happy bunny

Glossary

IThe Internet has its very own language (some would say jargon), much of it in the form of acronyms. If you want to make the most of the Web you do need to learn the basic terms.

@

In an e-mail address the @ sign (at) goes before the name of the provider of the mail box.

ADSL (ASYMETRIC DIGITAL SUBSCRIBER LINE)

This technology lets you transform an ordinary telephone line into a high speed line for transmitting digital data (500 kbps–2 mbps).

ALGORITHM

A set of mathematical rules used to perform a calculation or solve a problem.

ANALOGUE

The 'opposite' of digital – an analogue system encodes information using physical variables (eg electrical voltages, magnetism) whereas a digital system represents information with numbers.

BANDWIDTH

The amount of data that can be transported by means of a given communication channel. Normally measured in bits per second (bps).

BIT

The smallest unit of information handled by a computer. Data transfer speed is expressed in bits per second (bps).

BOOKMARK

With bookmarks you can save your favourite URL addresses in your browser and then easily retrieve the chosen sites when you need to – just like using a traditional bookmark to mark your page in a reading book.

CABLE

A network originally for television transmission, but which today transports (among other things) high speed Internet transmissions (512 kbps).

CACHE

Part of a hard disk which stores Web pages already visited, thus allowing faster retrieval.

CHAT

See IRC.

COMPRESSION

A way of reducing the size of data, by excluding anything which is not essential to recreate the original.

COOKIES

A small file created on your computer by a Website, and used as a 'tag' to help track and record your progress through the site. It is possible to refuse 'cookies'.

DOMAIN

The end of an Internet address. 'com' for commercial sites, 'uk' for the UK, 'fr' for France, 'jp' for Japan etc., 'org' for organisation, 'edu' for education.

DOWNLOAD

To transfer a file onto the hard disk of your computer.

E-MAIL

Electronic mail.

ENCRYPTION ALGORITHM

A mathematical process for encoding data.

FAQ

Frequently asked questions, or the ones everybody asks, with answers. Newcomers to sites or discussion groups should read the list of FAQs to avoid posing the same questions as everyone else.

FRAMES

Frames are used to display multi-window pages.

FREEWARE

Software made available for public use without any charge.

FTP (FILE TRANSFER PROTOCOL)

Internet file transfer protocol suitable for transferring large files.

GATEWAY

A bridge between two networks.

GIF, JPEG, PICT, TIFF

Graphics file formats used on the Internet. An animated GIF displays a sequence of images.

GSM

Global system for mobile communications.

GPRS

The General Packet Radio Service is a network that enables users to send data via mobile phones at higher speeds than previously possible under GSM.

HACKER

A computer pirate who infiltrates networks. The image of the typical hacker is usually someone young and clever.

HOME PAGE

A welcome page or front page of a site containing a summary of its contents and the first page you will see when logging onto the Internet.

HOTLINE

Technical help line offered by an Internet Service Provider or computer equipment supplier.

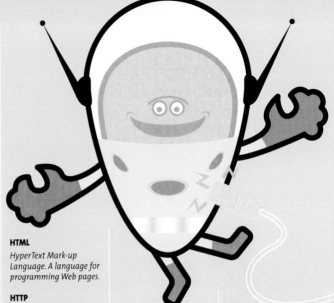

HTML

HyperText Mark-up Language. A language for programming Web pages.

HTTP

HyperText Transfer Protocol. The protocol used to access information on the Web.

HYPERTEXT

A system where Internet documents contain links to other documents (text, graphics etc.) The links make it easier to navigate your way around the Net.

INTEGRATED CIRCUIT

A miniature chip that has the functionality of several conventional components. They are the basis of most modern electrical and computerised devices.

INTERFACE

A hardware or software device used to enable communication between two computers or networks.

INTERNET

The Internet is an international network of computers linked up to exchange information using the Internet Protocol (IP). The Internet is a descendent of ARPANET, a military network founded in 1969.

INTERNET PROTOCOL (IP)

The system of uniquely identifying any computer or server connected to the Internet. IP is used with TCP to allow computers to exchange information over the Internet.

INTRANET

An Internet type network, but which is used internally by a company or organisation.

ICQ

'I seek you.' One of the main chat networks.

IRC (INTERNET RELAY CHAT)

A system where you can converse (in written form) directly on the Internet.

ISDN

Integrated Services Digital Network. A world-wide standard for the delivery of digital information over dual telephone lines at higher speed than conventional phone lines (at 64 or 128 kbps).

JAVA

Programming language developed by Sun Microsystems and commonly used for Web applications.

LINUX

A freely distributed operating system which is becoming more and more popular. A serious competitor for Windows, due to its stability and the fact that all the code for the operating system is 'open source',

ie available to anyone for alteration and improvement.

MAC

Short for Macintosh, the major alternative to PC compatibles that can be used to access the Internet. The Mac's operating system is Mac OS. Technically a Mac is also a PC though people tend to differentiate between the two, calling IBM machines PCs.

META-ENGINE

A super search engine which launches simultaneous searches using several engines.

MICROPROCESSOR

A microprocessor is an integrated circuit which contains all the functionality necessary to perform as a computer CPU (Central Processing Unit).

MIME (MULTIPURPOSE INTERNET MAIL EXTENSIONS

A system which allows you to read a document (text, graphics, sound etc.) attached to an e-mail message.

MODEM (MODULATOR-DEMODULATOR)

A computer peripheral allowing computers to communicate with one another over conventional telephone lines by converting digital data into analogue data and vice versa.

MODERATOR

Overseer or administrator of a newsgroup or chat-room. The moderator screens messages which are posted, and occasionally directs or prompts discussion.

MP3

An audio format that produces CD-quality audio – it is fast becoming the standard for transmitting music files on the Internet.

MPEG3 – MOVING PICTURE EXPERT GROUP LAYER 3

A format for the compression of video files.

NEWSGROUP

Discussion groups on chosen themes using written messages. See also Usenet.

OFF-LINE (NOT CONNECTED)

An off-line operation is one that can be carried

out without being connected to the network.

OPERATING SYSTEM

The head honcho of programmes on your computer. It controls and manages the other programmes installed on your computer. Microsoft Windows and MacOS are examples of operating systems.

PATENTED PUBLIC KEY

A security code used by encryption algorithm.

PC (PERSONAL COMPUTER)

A small computer commonly used for Internet access. PCs represent about 80 per cent of world sales. Most PCs are sold with Microsoft's Windows operating system pre-installed.

PERIPHERAL

An add-on to a computer, such as a printer, a modem or a scanner.

PLUG-IN

A small software programme that 'plugs in' to a browser to add functionality (eg Flash, Realplayer).

POP (POINT OF PRESENCE)

An Internet connection point. Providers have several Pops distributed

over their area, so keeping Internet users' telephone bills down.

PORTAL

A site which lets you access a string of other sites and offers services (information, weather forecasts etc.), search engines and even newsgroups. Yahoo! is probably the best known.

PPP (POINT TO POINT PROTOCOL)

Allows a computer to be connected to the Internet via a modem and an ordinary telephone line.

PROTOCOL

Set of computer standard rules used for performing a particular task (eg network protocol, file transfer protocol).

PROXY

A computer which stores the most frequently requested pages so that they can be recalled more quickly.

SERVER

A server is a powerful computer which provides files, data, applications or other services to any computers or users who connect to it. It is the basis of a network.

SHAREWARE

Software that is made available for a trial

period free of charge. If you decide to use it you then pay a fee to the authors.*

SITE

The name for any (virtual) place on the Internet.

SMILEYS

A set of characters used to express emotion or sentiment. Very popular in e-mails and IRC. Also known as emoticons.

SMTP (SIMPLE MAIL TRANSFER PROTOCOL)

E-mail transmission system.

TCP/IP (TRANSMISSION CONTROL PROTOCOL/INTERNET PROTOCOL)

Stands for Transfer Control Protocol/ Internet Protocol. TCP is the standard that computers use to transfer information across the Internet. IP is the standard used to uniquely identify any computer or server connected to the Internet.

TRANSISTOR

A transistor is a semiconductor which can amplify a signal – a simple electronic component which formed the basis of many electrical devices before integrated circuits were developed.

UNIX

A powerful operating system commonly used to run powerful network and Web servers.

URL (UNIFORM RESOURCE LOCATOR)

An Internet address. Addresses usually begin with www.

USENET

A newsgroup system (collection of computer networks) that exchange messages organised by subject.

WAP (WIRELESS APPLICATION PROTOCOL)

Technical standards governing connection of mobile telephones to the Internet.

WWW (WORLD WIDE WEB)

The Web, the multimedia part of the Internet.

WEB

Abbreviation of World Wide Web.

WEBMASTER

Person in charge of a Website.

WINDOWS

Microsoft operating system for PCs.

Software library

To browse the Web efficiently you need various pieces of software, each with a different function. Some are included in the provider's access package and others have to be downloaded, or purchased. Software is constantly being upgraded, and improved software will always need more memory in order to work properly, so on occasion you may have to perform updates. As time goes on you will build up a sizeable software library.

Shareware versus freeware

Freeware are programmes that have been copyrighted but are made available for public use without any charge. They can therefore be downloaded free.

Shareware are programmes to which copyright is attached that are also made available free of charge, but only for a trial period, at the end of which, if you like the programme you have to pay a fee to the programme's author to continue using it.

Browsers

Internet Explorer

Microsoft's classic Web browser. It can be downloaded from the Microsoft Website, for Mac or PC, from **www.microsoft.com**, but is pre-installed in many computers.

Netscape Navigator

Netscape Navigator is often considered easier to use than its great rival, Microsoft. There are versions for PC and for Mac, and it can be downloaded or bought on CD Rom for a modest sum. **www.netscape.com**

Anti-virus software

Norton

Norton is both a very popular virus detection and removal programme and a powerful tool

box to help you get to the heart of your computer, enabling you to optimise your hard drive and protect against systems crashes.

PC-cillin

Download a free 30-day trial version of PC-cillin 2000. Note that no anti-virus software is 100 per cent effective, as virus writers also have the programmes and devise new ways of getting round them. However, better safe than sorry. **www.antivirus.com/pc-cillin**

Sound and video

Real Player

Over time Real Player has become almost standard software for sound and video, and should be on the hard disk of every regular Internet user. **www.real.com**

Musicmatch

A classic MP3 reader, with a good graphics interface. The free player also lets you record CD quality audio. **www.musicmatch.com**

Sonique

This superb MP3 reader can also read Wav, mod and audio CD files and has a very good customisable interface. **www.sonique.com**

Cool Player

Introduced fairly recently, this nimble little MP3 reader is becoming more and more popular. **www.daansystems.com/coolplayer/**

Real Networks
The industry standard for video streaming over the Web (i.e. the software starts playing the video after only a few seconds, instead of waiting to download the entire file).
www.realnetworks.com

Win Amp
The best known of the MP3 readers which has practically become standard software and very easy to use. **www.winamp.com**

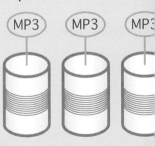

Note for Macintosh users. Downloadable software is sometimes provided exclusively for PC users. You should download Mac versions if they exist.

Further reading

Almost all bookshops have a computers and Internet section these days, so browsing the shelves might be the best way of finding out the latest publications. Online booksellers (eg. www amazon. co.uk, www. .bol.com) will also have a very wide selection covering all aspects of the Web, from guides to Web sites for children to romantic fiction set against an Internet background.

History

Tim Berners-Lee, *Weaving the Web*, Orion, 1999
Subtitled 'The past, present and future of the World
Wide Web' and written by one of the Net's pioneers.

Katie Hafner, Matthew Lyon, *Where Wizards Stay Up
Late*, Simon & Schuster, 1998
A well-researched account, including interviews with
some of the Internet's inventors.

John Naughton, *A Brief History of the Future*, Phoenix
Press, 2000
An in-depth history, going back to the Internet's
precedents in the 1930s. Naughton neglects neither the
technological advances nor the human achievements
behind them.

Guides

Parry Aftab, *The Parent's Guide to Protecting Children in
Cyberspace*, McGraw-Hill, 2000

Alliance for Technological Access, *Computer and Web
Resources for People with Disabilities*, Hunter House,
2000

Patrick Beuzit, *Creating Your Own Web Site with
FrontPage Express*, Cassell & Co, 2001

Graham Edmonds, *The Good Web Site Guide 2001*, Orion

Angus J. Kennedy, *Rough Guide to the Internet*, 2001

Jean-Pierre Lovinfosse, *HTML*, Cassell & Co, 2000
For those with only basic knowledge of HTML, or
complete beginners.

Franck Marc, *Internet Explorer 5: A Simple Guide for
Beginners*, Cassell & Co, 2000

Mark S. Merkow, James Breithaupt, *The Complete Guide
to Internet Security*, McGraw-Hill, 2000

Jean-Paul Mesters, *Real-time Communication on the
Internet: Live Chat & Instant Messaging with IRC and ICQ*,
Cassell & Co, 2000

Mark Neely, *The Complete Beginner's Guide to the
Internet*, Net Works, 1999

Philip Treleaven, *The Sunday Times 'E-business St@rt-up':
The Complete Guide to Launching Your Internet and
Digital Enterprise*, 2000

Virga, *E-mail*, Cassell & Co, 2000
Discusses e-mail techniques and the characteristics of
the most widely used e-mail software brands.

Lynda Weinmann, *Dreamweaver 3 Hands-On Training*,
Peachpit Press, 2000

Security

Bernard Fabrot, *Security Online*, Cassell & Co, 2001
A pocket guide to a subject that should concern all
Internet users, especially anyone who makes purchases
online.

Clive Walker (editor), *Crime, Criminal Justice and the
Internet*, Sweet & Maxwell, 1998
A more detailed study of Internet crime.

Fiction

William Gibson, *Neuromancer*, Voyager, 1989 A science
fiction novel that introduces the concept of 'cyberspace'.

Susan Taggart, *Web of Intrigue*, Bethany House, 1998
A murder investigation draws Morgan Carruthers
through some of the darker passages of the Web.

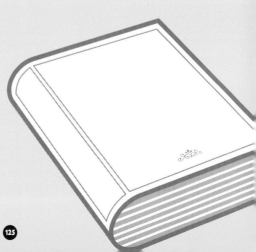

Contents

Fact ⟩⟩ 2–12
Fun facts and quick quotes

Discover ⟩⟩ 13–50

Look ⟫ 51–68

The Web has given an interesting twist to everyday words

In practice ⟫ 69–100

Find out ⟫ 101–128

Acknowledgements

P.16, Eniac, the first computer, built in Pennsylvania (1943-1946), Los Alamos National Library/Science Photo Library – **P.19**, World Wide Web © Mehau Kulyk/Science Photo Library – **P.20**, Volume of information transmitted between the United States and other countries in November 1994, © Mehau Kulyk/Science Photo Library – **P.23**, © Fontshop – **P.24**, Electronic stock market display on a building in Times Square, © Tony Craddock/Science Photo Library – **P.28,** © Tony Craddock/Science Photo Library – **P.31,** © Fontshop – **P.32**, Le bus Internet, © Benoit Decout/REA Seine Maritime – **P.35**, © Vision/Popperfoto/Cosmos – **P.36** © David Gifford/Science Photo Library – **P.39**, © Fontshop – **P.40**, © Fontshop – **P.43**, © Fontshop – **P.44**, Internet en Ardèche © Eric Franceschi/Agence VU – **P.47**, La maison du futur, Vilvoorde Belgique © Van Parys Media Sygma – **P.48**, © la S.E.F.T.I (service d'enquête fraudes aux technologies de l'information) © Alain Nogues/Sygma – **P.52**, © Eiichi Anzai – **P.53**, Surfeurs © Ph. Research/Sunstar/Explorer – **P.54**, © Ross Rappaport/Photonica – **P.56**, © Philippe Roy/Explorer – **P.57**, Abeille butineuse, © D. Bringard/Explorer – **P.58**, © Ko Fujiwara/Photonica – **P.59**, © H. Horenstein/Photonica – **P.60**, © Grandordy/Explorer – **P.61**, © Fontshop – **P.62**, Maison, © William Huber/Photonica – **P.63**, Village de Saint-Flour, France, © Patrick Chazot/Explorer – **P.64**, Pont suspendu, © Christophe Boisvieux/Explorer – **P.65**, © T.Nakajima/Photonica – **P.66**, © Ima Kerama/Photonica – **P.67**, © Ch.Bjornberg /Ph. Rese/Explorer – **P.68**, © P. MCDonough/Photonica – **P.70–100**, Infographies : Jacques Partouche – **P.102–125**, Illustrations : Phong Luong Dien.